# #BeCourageous

Meghan McCobb
Kate McCobb
Jennifer Kauffman

10-10-10
Publishing

Publisher
10-10-10 Publishing
Markham, ON  Canada

Printed in Canada and the United States of America

# Contents

# Praise

"As someone who grew up with low-grade depression and who struggled to fit in, I found this book fascinating and uplifting. Any child or young adult will relate, no matter what their challenges have been. #BeCourageous is filled with inspirational messages, courageous concepts, and stories that will simply leave you in awe."

**Marci Shimoff**
**Featured Teacher for the movie The Secret**
**Best-Selling Author of Happy For No Reason and Love For No Reason**
**Co-Founder of Your Year of Miracles Program**

"Having worked with thousands of people, I have come to know that we all have been harmed. We don't have the freedom to choose what happens to us that leaves us traumatized. However, we have the power to turn the most horrendous acts of harm into the gift we give to the world.

The vulnerability and generosity these young authors model in sharing their stories will undoubtedly become an inspiration to other young people giving them hope to live – to fully live beyond whatever happened to them."

**Leila Reyes, MSW**
**Transformational Coach, facilitating the remembering of your wholeness**

"These honest and meaningful stories reveal what real courage is all about. We can learn through the wisdom and experience of the amazing authors and most importantly, be inspired to act on what's important and needed right now."

**Marcia Wieder, CEO**
**Dream University and best-selling author**

"#BeCourageous is an important read for all kids and families growing up in today's world. These simple, yet profound stories illustrate powerful life lessons that I wish I had learned as a child. It is humbling to see so many young people sharing their stories, how they shifted their mindset to successfully move through stressful times and come out stronger on the other side.

The authors' illustrations and word play enable big concepts to be easily accessible for children and people of all ages. I loved how the chapters build on each other with a beautiful summation of the concepts with real strategies to create the best quality life.

As a professional who has worked over 30 years with children challenged by learning differences, I thank you for writing this book."

**Pam Formosa, MA OTR/L**
**Founder: Brain Fit Academy, Inc.**
**Author: FRAID NOT! Empowering Kids with**
**Learning Differences**

"Jennifer Kauffman, Meghan and Kate McCobb do an "inspiring" job on their new book, #BeCourageous. They each share some of their own personal stories and how they were able to overcome those challenges. There are also examples faced by others with situations and key concepts to help "RISE" above each challenge.

The book is thoughtfully written and done in such a way that all are able to read and can connect with. Each chapter contains personal stories in which they share the challenges they each faced with the reader and offer key concepts in how to possibly deal with the challenge and help move on. You will continue to read and reread each and every chapter. You will identify the concepts that most interest and relate to you but, I believe that this book will give you the courage to RISE above any situation you are facing.

I highly recommend this book for parents and children to read together, for teachers to share with students, for guidance counselors to reflect with students and for anyone facing a challenge who needs some support and guidance to be able to move forward. Be strong, be you, and FLY!

**Jan Maglione ~ Teacher and Member of The Massachusetts Readers Council**

"Children, especially teenagers more than ever need to develop resilience and self-regulation skills. It's crucial for them to know that there are answers and they are not alone. Kudos to the brave kids that shared their stories in this book. "Be Courageous" promotes the importance of mindset, attitude and communication. All valuable skills for success in the 21st century."

**Sheena L. Smith ~ Speaker, Author "All Kids Can Thrive"**

"When I was given the manuscript of #BeCourageous, I thought I would read a bit of it so that I could give Jennifer, Kate and Meghan some helpful feedback--but I ended up not being able to put it down. There is so much knowledge and richness in this book, not only for young teens but for everyone. I recommend that families read it together and discuss and share their thoughts about each chapter and each concept. It will be a game changer for your life and a way to connect with each other around some of today's most important issues."

**Debra Poneman, Bestselling author and founder Yes to Success, Inc.**

We dedicate this book to our wonderful grandmothers: Nan, who passed away in 2018, and Grammy, who is an amazing grandmother. Our grandmothers play such an important role in our lives, because they are always there for us, and they help us whenever we need it most.

We also dedicate this book to our extraordinary mom and dad. They are so special to us, and they make our lives so amazing! We simply don't have any words to describe them best, since they are so loving!

Lastly, we dedicate this book to the most amazing aunt, who made this book happen! Whenever we need something, she's there for us; she is always looking out for us, and we are very thankful for her.

~Kate and Meghan McCobb~

# With Love and Gratitude

*"Gratitude is the healthiest of all human emotions.*
*The more you express gratitude for what you have,*
*the more likely you will have even more*
*to express gratitude for."*
~Zig Ziglar~

We have been truly blessed to be given such an incredible opportunity to write our very first book with our Auntie Jennifer. Our Auntie Jennifer taught us the process of writing a book, as well as introducing us to some extraordinarily successful people, who were gracious enough to allow us to interview them. She taught us how to prepare for and encouraged us to lead the interviews, where we learned so many powerful lessons and empowering insights, which are captured in this book. We are really lucky to have been given this wonderful opportunity. Thank you, Auntie!

We would like to thank our mom and dad, and Grammy, for supporting us through the process of writing our first book, and for encouraging us every step of the way. They spent countless hours reading and re-reading our book to ensure that it was the best it could be. It is because of their dedication and commitment that we were able to complete this powerful and inspirational book.

We would also like to give a special thank you to the extraordinary women who allowed us to interview them so we could include their wisdom in our book: **Marci Shimoff**, #1 *New York Times* best-selling author and world renowned transformational teacher and expert on happiness, success, and unconditional love; **Debra Poneman**, considered a pioneer in the field of personal growth, and founder of the YES to Success program; and **Iris Polit**, a career transition and personal branding strategist and bestselling author, who is certified in applied positive psychology. Iris taught us about positive psychology and the importance of mindset when dealing with a traumatic experience. These women gave us an opportunity to learn how to interview successful people, as well as to capture their golden nuggets of wisdom so that kids like us could understand what they teach to adults every day.

We want to give a big thank you to our wonderful editor, **Shauna Hardy**, who helped us bring our idea of Iris Donahue, the narrator of our book, to life. We are very grateful for all her help in making this book what it is today.

We want to thank the wonderful moms, dads, and siblings who spent countless hours helping their children write their inspirational stories for our book.

We would like to give a big shout out to all the amazing young authors who participated in our book: **Dmitri Krasnov, Arlene Coleman, Raven Reitano, Amanda Blake, and Marissa and Julia Gallego**. We thank you for your courage and bravery in writing your very personal stories. Our hope is that your stories will inspire and encourage many other kids and their parents to realize that they, too, can rise above any challenge in life. To learn more about these courageous and amazing young authors, please visit www.becourageousbook.com.

We would like to thank **Raymond Aaron** and his entire team for helping us publish our first book. This has been a challenging and rewarding experience for us.

We are so blessed and extremely grateful for this amazing experience, and we truly hope that our book inspires and encourages lots of people around the world!

## Gratitude brings us happiness!

# About Meghan, Kate, and "Auntie" Jennifer

**Meghan** is now age 13, and was 12 when she started writing this book. Meghan is musically gifted, and loves basketball and field hockey. At the age of 9, she shared the stage with Kristen Merlin, who finished in the top 5 of *The Voice*. Meghan and Kristen sang "Blank Space," a Taylor Swift song. Meghan is an alter server at her church, and she has a passion for helping kids less fortunate than her. She is choosing to donate a portion of the book proceeds to https://www.stjude.org/give.html.

**Kate** is now age 11, and was 10 when she started writing this book. Kate loves Harry Potter, gymnastics, and doing anything fun. Kate is adventurous and a natural born leader. She consistently meets or exceeds her Girl Scout fundraising goals, earning her over 50 badges. Kate has a passion for animals, particularly dogs. She is choosing to donate a portion of the book proceeds to https://bestfriends.org/.

**Jennifer** is Meghan's and Kate's aunt, who thought it would be a brilliant idea to gift her nieces with an opportunity to write their very first book. Writing a book is not easy, and she thought this experience would be a building block for future successes in their lives. Jennifer is an award-winning results coach; best-selling author; executive producer of the Emmy and Telly Award-winning documentary, *A New Leash on Life: The K9's for Warriors Story;* and a survivor of the 2013 Boston Marathon bombings. Jennifer is also an inspirational and transformational speaker and teacher. Jennifer is passionate about helping people, including children, rise above their challenges so that they can live their best lives! While working with Meghan and Kate, as well as all the amazing young authors in this book, she found the experience to be so fulfilling and rewarding. She was fortunate to teach the young authors what it means to be happy for no reason, along with life-altering success principles and courageous key concepts, many of which she only learned as an adult. To see these young authors absorb these concepts was simply awe-inspiring for her!

# Foreword

Have you or someone you love ever experienced a traumatic or very challenging situation? The book you are about to read is filled with short inspirational stories from children and young adults who have gone through some extremely challenging times. Rather than being defined as a victim of their experiences, these young authors were able to rise above them, and become even stronger as a result. They truly were able to transform themselves, and they all became victors instead of victims.

You have the power to do this too—no matter what your current circumstance or situation is. Within the pages of this book, the authors share inspiring and powerful messages of hope, which can help you rise above any challenge.

Remember, life is always going to throw you curve balls —the key to rising above them is to develop the core life principles that are outlined in this book.

As you read #BeCourageous, notice what resonates for you; notice the courageous key concepts you are drawn to and ask yourself, "Which ones do I want to apply in my life starting now?" It is through applying the concepts that resonate for you that you'll be able to create a more energized, powerful and extraordinary life.

Get ready to go on a transformational adventure!

My wish for you is that this book will inspire and empower you to rise above any challenging situation, so you can create a life filled with inner peace, love, joy and happiness.

**Raymond Aaron**
**New York Times Bestselling Author**

# Courageous Beginnings
by Iris Donohue

*"Courage is resistance to fear, mastery of fear—
not the absence of fear."*
~Mark Twain~

Hello, I'm Iris Donahue, the narrator of this book—a series of inspirational stories, written by kids and teenagers, who've lived through some really tough times and found a way to break through their fears. My hope is that you will be inspired and encouraged, as well as know that you, too, can do anything you set your mind to! Anything is possible as long as you believe.

**"Happiness can be found even in the
darkest of times if one only
remembers to turn on the light"
~Albus Dumbledore~**

In each chapter, I will introduce the author, highlight their inspiring message, and share some powerful insights so that you, too, can learn to be courageous. Let's start with a courageous insight and a powerful word: *focus*. *Focus* is super important because it keeps you on track. Everything you focus on expands, so I encourage you to focus on the positive and uplifting messages sprinkled throughout this book. These messages, if you apply them in your own life, will help you in any situation. This book is intended to remind you not to dwell on the bad things that happen in life but instead to focus on the good in *all* experiences—and to find a way to courageously move forward.

**Each experience in life gives you a choice...**
**To be bitter or better.**
**We hope you choose better!**

Trauma has different shapes and sizes, and can happen any time in life. Trauma can mean different things to different people. A traumatic experience can include being left alone when you didn't feel ready, or being bullied by someone, or losing a sibling, parent, or grandparent. It could be learning that you or a loved one has a serious illness, or you are losing your home and all your material possessions; or you were going after an important goal/dream of yours, and you didn't achieve it the first time. The point is to not compare your trauma to anyone else's. The truth is that every person on the planet goes through traumatic experiences...that's life! These experiences are intended to bring out the best in you, if you allow it. Again, notice where you have the choice to be bitter or better for having gone through the difficult experience.

The diagram below illustrates the power you have within you to choose how you respond to difficult situations. If the situation leaves you *bitter,* then you are likely spiraling down and out of control. You are likely in a state of frustration, worry, doubt, resentment, anger, jealousy, and maybe even hatred, all of which are considered *victim mentality.* The opposite is true if you choose to see each challenge/difficult experience as an opportunity to expand and grow; then you will respond differently. You will be rising up to your best self...notice how the upward spiral is filled with optimism, hope, enthusiasm, joy, love, and happiness. This is

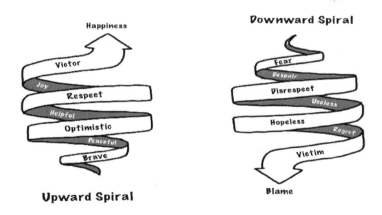

**Energy Chart**

M. McCabe

considered a *victor mentality*. Each person has a choice to be a victim or a victor. You will learn more about being a victim and victor, as you read this powerful book.

The key to living a courageous and successful life starts on the inside...how do you see yourself? Do you see yourself as broken, as illustrated below? Or do you see yourself as a lion, who is strong, courageous, and fearless? You have the power inside of you to transform yourself from feeling broken to being empowered. It's all up to you to choose how you want to live your life!

**Broken...**          Or          **Strong & Courageous**

# Chapter 1

## Bouncing Back
## After Losing Everything
by Dmitri Krasnov

*"Every test in our life makes us bitter or
BETTER...Every problem comes to MAKE us
or break us...The choice is ours whether
we become a victim or VICTOR."*
~Rishika Jain~

**Iris:** When you look at your life, would you say that you are a victor or a victim? People who have a victim mentality constantly whine and complain about what is happening in their lives. Nothing is ever good enough for them. Victims blame everyone for their problems, and they are typically difficult to be around. Victors, on the other hand, are people who embrace every challenge and problem they encounter; they see problems as positive situations to help them grow.

If we are not growing, then we are slowly dying. Each day gives us an opportunity to be a victor, to expand and flourish. Being a victor, and being around victors, will help you grow even faster. Victors support and encourage each other; they are excellent at celebrating their progress, and even their failures. They look at disappointment as something positive and good—it means they have stepped outside their comfort zone and are attempting something new.

Remember when you learned to ride a bike? You didn't just jump on for the first time and ride it perfectly. You fell, repeatedly. You had to keep trying, and you didn't give up until you learned how to balance yourself. This is what it means to be a victor. It means never giving up until you've reached your goal.

When he was only 7 years old, Dmitri faced a devastating loss...his home burned down. As you read about his experience, see if you can spot which mentality Dmitri chooses.

*Is he a victim or a victor?*

\* \* \*

*Hello, my name is Dmitri. I am 10 years old; I love playing soccer, and I like swimming. I live in Florida now, but the story I am going to tell, happened when I lived in Massachusetts.*

*One night, after everyone had gone to sleep (my mom was out of the house, working a shift at a café), my grandma woke up because of a strange dripping sound. It was two o'clock in the morning, and when she tried to turn on the light, she noticed the wall around the light switch was warm. My grandma went to check on a little storage room next to her bedroom, and when she opened the door, smoke and fire came pouring from the room.*

*We called the police right away, and my dad told my brother to grab a fire extinguisher. My dad tried to put out the fire, but it was too big. We knew it was too dangerous to stay in the house, so we went outside. Our cat, Zorra, was still in the house, and we were very worried about her. The rest of my home was already on fire, and we had no idea where Zorra could be. The firefighters went inside the house, but they couldn't find our cat. I was really scared and nervous.*

*Our house caught fire in February, and the weather was super cold. We didn't have time to grab our coats, and we got really cold. We were so grateful when we saw that an ambulance had come to save us from the freezing weather. Thank God, everyone was safe and no one was hurt.*

*The next day, we went back to my house to search for our cat. When we walked up to the top floor of the house, we were scared that we would fall right through the floorboards. Luckily, nothing happened, and we found our cat! She was hiding outside under our balcony.*

*I still don't know how our house caught on fire, but the most important thing is that we are all alive.*

\* \* \*

**Iris:** Even though Dmitri is very sad over the loss of his house, you will notice that he expressed lots of gratitude: for being alive, for finding his cat, for the ambulance that kept him warm. Gratitude is a very important part of being a victor. When Dmitri shares his experience, he doesn't just focus on the sadness of the situation; he embraces the good that occurred. We can do this in any circumstance—no matter how challenging. What are you grateful for right now? How does being grateful make you feel?

**Thoughts + Feelings + Actions = Results**

Do you think this equation is true or false? The answer is true. All of your thoughts, feelings, and actions equal the results that you see in your life. There are two versions:

Negative Thoughts + Icky Feelings + Poor Decisions or Inaction = Disappointing Results

**or**

**Positive Thoughts + Uplifting Feelings + Massive Action = Miraculous Results**

Dmitri is currently at a crossroads when it comes to these equations. At 10 years old, he is grateful that he and his loved ones were saved, and yet he struggles with sadness and disappointment over losing his home and all of his possessions. He is also displeased over his family's choices. Rather than rebuild their home, they decided to move to Florida instead.

**"Let go of expectations.**
**Let go of your attachment to outcomes."**
**Livelifehappy.com**

When trauma occurs, it's easy to slip into the victim mentality, to embrace negative thoughts and icky feelings, and make unintentional decisions that aren't in our best interests. It's completely normal for all of us to go back and forth between being a victim and a victor, between the negative equation and the positive one. It's all a matter of where we put our focus.

Dmitri has a choice about whether he continues to harbor these negative feelings of anger and resentment that will create more and more distance from those he loves. His other choice is to forgive, and to focus on his new dream of one day returning to Massachusetts and rebuilding his home. One equation leads him to a disappointing life, while the other equation allows him to expand and soar in life.

## The Power of YET

Have you ever felt disappointed, like Dmitri did when he lost his home and all of his possessions? Have you felt like you kept trying to do something, and it simply wasn't working? Have you ever noticed yourself saying any of these disempowering statements?

"Why is this happening to me?" or "Why me?"
"I can't do this; I quit..."
"This isn't working; I give up..."

You have the power within you to go from being disempowered to empowered. Disempowered is where you choose to give away your power, and you ultimately feel hopeless. Empowered is where you choose to take your power back. It's where you unleash the warrior part of you, who will keep going for it until you achieve your desired goal. Warriors never quit, no matter how challenging the situation is; they always find a way to rise up stronger, more powerful and loving. They see challenges as opportunities to grow!

When you are feeling discouraged, pause for a few minutes and take several deep breaths. Even go for a walk outside. It is amazing how much a walk outdoors can make us feel better. After you take a pause, train your brain to ask empowering questions, and say powerful statements to yourself. How you talk to your self during difficult times will determine if you are a victim or victor. I'm sure you are asking yourself how do you do that. Here's how; train your mind to ask or say any of the following empowering questions and statements:

"What can I learn from this experience?"
"What good can come from this difficult situation?"
"In time, I will be able to do this," or tell yourself,
"I can and will do this someday!"
"I will keep going for it until I succeed!"
"Just do it! Just keep moving forward!"

Now, take a few more deep breaths, read aloud the *disempowering* phrases on the previous page, and then notice how you feel. Do the disempowering statements make you feel down and powerless?

Take a few more deep breaths, read the *empowering* questions and statements above, and notice how you feel. Do the empowering statements light a spark inside of you? Do you feel more hopeful and maybe even a little more courageous? Remember, you have the power within you to go from being disempowered to empowered, and once you do, we encourage you to go for your goals and dreams!

**No One Can Make You Feel Inferior Unless You Allow Them!**

# Chapter 2

## Weathering the Tempest
by Arlene Coleman

*"We seem to think that our character is defined by our experiences, but rather I have come to understand that our experiences are defined by our character."*
~Arlene Coleman~

**Iris:** "I am brave. I am strong. I am brave ... oh wait, I just said that ... maybe because I AM BRAVE!" You are, too, in your own way.

Did you know that everyone has important moments in their lives where they are called upon to be brave? Think back on your life so far. When did it happen for you? Was it speaking up when you saw someone being bullied? Or did it happen when you gave your presentation in front of the class, even though you happen to be very shy? Bravery has different faces— sometimes it's about trying something new; sometimes it's about facing something that scares us.

Arlene had to be very brave when she was just a young child. After losing her home, she immigrated to a new country, with her family, in order to build a safer, happier life. Facing an unfamiliar situation required Arlene to be extremely courageous.

Being brave often goes hand in hand with facing something that scares you. Most people I know are afraid of fear and do everything to avoid it. I've learned that actually embracing my fears is much more effective. It means I am trying new things, which ultimately helps me grow. Think of fear as:

**Face Everything And R** I S E

**Tips to embracing your fears:**

Acknowledge your fears. Speak your fears, either to yourself or to someone you trust. Remember that fear is a normal reaction, and it is very useful in our lives. Learning how to feel, assess, and respond to your fear is a very important skill that you will use for the rest of your life. Listen to what it is telling you, and then keep moving toward your goal. Let fear guide you, not drive you! Always remember that you are in charge of what you want to achieve in life!

Take the first step to breaking through your fear. Arlene could have let the fear of her new situation completely overwhelm her. Instead, she took small steps each day to become more and more comfortable with her new life. Starting with small steps allows you to build up your courage and confidence.

Don't forget to celebrate your progress along the way. The more you celebrate your achievements (both big and small), the more confident and courageous you'll become, which will empower you to keep taking positive actions.

I hope that you are inspired by Arlene's story of bravery. It contains important lessons that you'll be able to use in your own life!

**"You're going to go through tough times—that's life. But I say, 'Nothing happens to you, it happens for you.' See the positive in negative events."**
**~Joel Osteen~**

* * *

*Hi, I am Arlene, and I am going through a personal storm, at age 21, which I did not expect. A loved one, suffering with a mental illness, has made choices that have directly impacted my financial and emotional stability. It has uprooted my life and drastically changed the future I had envisioned. This is an experience that has brought up questions and doubts about my path through life that I once thought was sure-footed and stable.*

**"Everything you want
is on the other side of fear"
~Jack Canfield~**

*It has directed me back to the basics, back to my roots. There are lessons that I didn't even realize I had learned, and that have provided a strength through this recent storm; and it is because of an experience I had when I was very young—an experience that would shape and alter the rest of my life.*

**Backstory**
*I was born in Zimbabwe, a country in Southern Africa, which has been fraught with political unrest and danger for longer than I have been alive. I grew up with a 12-foot electric fence to keep others out, and a guard at the gate. My father slept with a revolver next to his bed, and there were bars on every window; and these things made us feel secure. The idea that we weren't safe, and that this wasn't a normal way of life, never occurred to me— because that was all I knew. But it wasn't always that way. My dad was born and raised in Zimbabwe, my mom in South*

*Africa, and their whole family and life was there. In 1987, Robert Mugabe was elected as president and began his 30-year authoritarian reign. The economic decline began in 1990, with political unrest starting shortly thereafter.*

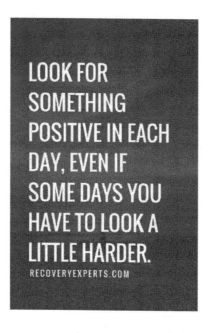

LOOK FOR SOMETHING POSITIVE IN EACH DAY, EVEN IF SOME DAYS YOU HAVE TO LOOK A LITTLE HARDER.

RECOVERYEXPERTS.COM

*Over the next few years, as the situation became worse, the views of the leadership began to influence the people, and tensions grew to a breaking point between the native population and those of European decent and other minorities. Those in power blamed minorities, such as the white farmers and the LGBTQ+ community, for many of Zimbabwe's problems. The situation grew worse; crime became increasingly rampant, and the army and police force became more corrupt. The government passed a land reform act that allowed them to forcibly take the land, homes, and property of anyone with European ancestry; and by 2013, every white-owned farm had been repossessed, including ours. When I was four, my mother, brother, and I were held up at gunpoint. Men that we referred to as "war vets" were looking for my father but found us instead. Trapped inside a little store on the edge of our property, with only one barred window and one door, the men blocked the only exit. Our bodyguard and garden boy pleaded with the men for over an hour to spare our lives. My mother radioed the police, but they wouldn't come to our aid because it was a political situation, and they refused to get involved. When the men finally let us go, we fled back to our farmhouse, inside the safety of our guarded fence. My father met us there, and the gates now seemed a flimsy barrier between us and the men that stood and chanted outside our gates all night long. Not long after that, we had to leave our home in fear of losing our lives. These things seem as foreign to me now as they do to most people that have only ever lived in a safe, free country. Sometimes, when I tell others about my experience, it feels like someone else's story, but these events played a big part in my life once upon a time, and altered the course of my life forever.*

*After we lost our home, with the help of others, we found ourselves thousands of miles away from Zimbabwe, in a new country, with a new language and a new culture. My brother and I were lucky; many memories faded quickly, and we were young enough that the culture shock and language barrier didn't last long. My parents were so grateful to be in Canada, in a country with more opportunity and freedom than we had ever known. They instilled a thankfulness in us that helped to outweigh the pangs of homesickness; and those days when we were just weary of the continual winter cold, a gratitude bigger than any sadness or anger for our losses. I will be forever appreciative of the way my parents' outlook on the situation shaped my mindset and emotional perspective.*

### The Tempest in the Teacup

**"I am not a product of my circumstances.
I am a product of my decisions."
~Stephen Covey~**

*I believe that everyone will face situations that are out of their control, like being bullied, or experiencing a death of a loved one. There are many things I have no say in, but I can choose my outlook on the situation, and that will make a difference.*

*Recently, I was reminded of the analogy of a teacup: I may not be able to control what happens to the cup; it may be bumped, chipped, or dropped, and when these things happen, whatever is in the cup may spill out. If there was milk in the cup, then milk may spill out; if there was coffee, then coffee may spill out. The external force on the cup doesn't change what is inside. It may be difficult to accept an adverse situation that was not caused by something I did, that was not my fault. I lost everything and was threatened and forced out of my home because of the color of my skin. The situation didn't arise as a consequence of my actions; it was totally out of my control.*

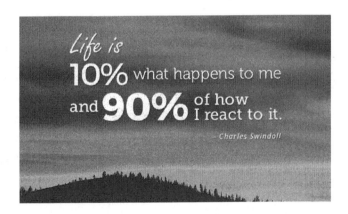

*It is easy to blame my foul mood on the situation, but I am responsible for the condition of my own mind. That doesn't necessarily make it any easier to face the experience, but it helps me have a more positive*

*outlook on a situation that might otherwise seem hopeless and empty. I have learned valuable lessons in some of the darkest moments of my life. The storm will eventually pass, no matter what it is, but I get to choose what I do with it. I get to choose to find the value in the experience, instead of giving into resentment, bitterness, or anger—I have the power to choose my reaction. This knowledge has helped me to see that I have a say in my future, even when events are out of my control.*

### *Finding Your Passion*

**"Success is no accident. It is hard work, perseverance, learning, studying, sacrifice, and most of all, love of what you are doing or learning to do."**
**~Pele~**

*When I was eight, we moved again, from Manitoba to Alberta. It was a time in my life that was full of anger, resentment, and bitterness. I felt I was just getting settled in our new life in Canada; I was making friends and becoming comfortable in the little town where we lived. Now that I am older, I understand the reason behind moving to Alberta; but at the time, it felt unexpected, and as though my parents were making this decision with no thought as to how my brother and I felt about it. When we arrived in Alberta, my parents started their own business, which introduced an enormous amount of additional and different stress into our family. I started a new school and had trouble making friends. It was a dark time, and I didn't understand why my life had been uprooted again. I felt I had no control over the situation; I became resentful of my parents for putting me in this situation, and I spent a lot of time wishing for something different. When I was eleven, I found a passion for writing. I used this passion as an outlet for the emotions I had not previously known how to articulate. Even if I wasn't writing about my experience, I used poetry and short stories as a creative outlet to release my pent-up feelings. Finding an outlet was great for two reasons: It gave me purpose, something I could do, something I enjoyed doing. And it gave me a way to express myself, a way to process my emotions, which in turn enabled me to let go of them and move on. Finding my passion was freeing and therapeutic; it gave me direction when I had never felt so lost.*

*Writing wasn't something I had done before, and it didn't matter if I did it well or badly. I had found something I could pour my heart and soul into, and it gave voice to my emotions.*

### The Danger of Loneliness

**"The worst part of holding the memories is
not the pain. It's the loneliness of it.
Memories need to be shared."
~Lois Lowry, The Giver~**

*One of the biggest contributing factors to my struggle,
when we moved to Alberta, was loneliness. I felt
isolated, alone in my misery, and these feelings fueled
a growing depression. If I had confided in my family,
I would have found out that my mom was feeling a
tremendous loss from moving, and that my dad was
feeling stressed and discouraged with the new
business.*

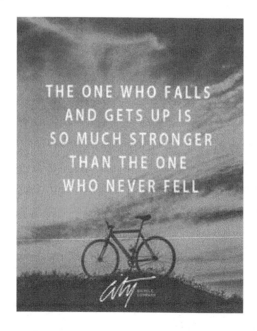

*I would have learned that my brother wasn't fitting in very well at our new school either. If I had shared my feelings, I would have had the opportunity to realize that I was not alone. I could have recognized that my feelings were normal and that it was okay to be sad for a time. We could have supported each other. In meeting the challenges of my current life, talking to others has opened my eyes to how many people deal with similar situations or emotions. Not that I want to dwell in my misery, but it is good to share what I am dealing with, and to understand I am not alone. It has helped me to feel stronger. I have been more able to face my present experiences with positivity and certainty that I will be okay. Finding someone to speak to about how I am feeling and what I am going through is a valuable tool that I did not have when I was younger.*

*Having someone I can share with freely, helps me to feel connected and supported in challenging situations; whether it's a friend, family member, teacher, or counselor. And there is power and encouragement in knowing that someone else has been able to overcome what I am facing. It is good to have proof that it does get better, and that somewhere, sometime, somehow, I will be okay again.*

### *The After*

**"Character cannot be developed in ease and quiet. Only through experience of trial and suffering can the soul be strengthened, ambition inspired, and success achieved."**
**~Helen Keller~**

*A huge part of moving forward has been learning to forgive. Until recently, I thought forgiveness was your response when someone apologized for something they had done. I am now beginning to understand that my forgiveness has little to do with the other person (or people) involved. To forgive is to set myself free from the negative emotions and thoughts associated with a person or the situation. It is about letting go and healing myself.*

*Whether the other party is sorry, it has no impact on my own ability to move forward. I once heard that holding a grudge is like drinking poison and expecting the other person to die. When I hold onto the negativity that another person has caused, it only hurts me. It is especially hard to feel compassion and love when I am in a difficult circumstance attributable to another person's choices. Forgiveness is a process, not an outcome; it requires patience with myself. I learn to let go a little more every day.*

*I accept that this will not happen all at once; I realize that it takes time to truly forgive, and it is for my own healing, not for the other person.*

*While I would never have wished for the things I have gone through, I am so thankful for the value that came from the experiences I faced. There are a lot of lessons that have helped me be successful in school, the workplace, and relationships. There are several people that have been great role models and sources of encouragement. I am hopeful that I will be a friend or advisor to someone else who is facing a tempest. I can be a source of hope and strength to someone else. I can show them that I have survived when I did not think it was possible. Every day, I have the opportunity to speak with people about my experience, and bring light to important issues such as discrimination and mental illness.*

*As part of the next generation, I am a teacher, leader, and voice of the future. Recognizing how issues have affected me and those I love, I have the amazing opportunity to influence my world. I use my voice and the strength of my experience to spur people on to be the change they want to see in the world.*

*It is possible that the most difficult experience you will ever face can bring out the very best in you. In the purification process of gold, it goes through the fire to be molded and shaped into something beautiful. You have the hope of being something more than what you once were, of using the trials you face for the betterment of yourself, and you can help someone else.*

*This knowledge provides me with a wonderful sense of purpose, a sense of direction that there is a way through, and that on the other side I can emerge stronger. Passing through my current storm, I know I am capable and well prepared, because I have already been through a life-changing challenge, and I survived. I am a better person for what I have faced; it has given me tools that make me courageous, and which support a successful outcome.*

*I truly believe that my perspective shapes my experience more than the external circumstances. There are a lot of factors that are outside of my control.*

*Life does not always seem fair, and I can find myself in situations I would not choose. I get to choose what I do with it; I get to choose to see the positive and to use the experience for my own betterment. I choose my attitude, my perspective, and how I will let external events affect the rest of my life.*

\* \* \*

**Iris:** When life hands you a challenging situation, what spills out of your teacup? Is it anger and resentment at the events that are occurring? Is it loneliness and despair? Or is it acceptance, curiosity, and gratitude?

Life boils down to the choices we make, and the way that we look at things. If you choose to embrace your circumstances with positivity, you will find a path filled with opportunity, love, joy, ease, and grace. But if you choose to look at life as if it's out to get you— that you've been handed a raw deal—you're surrounding yourself with a black cloud of negativity that will only make situations worse. What you focus upon expands and grows, so be sure to focus on the good in every situation, especially during the challenging times.

Your thoughts are like a playlist. If your playlist is playing nothing but sad, depressing music, it's time to find a new playlist. Right now! When your mind is stuck in a loop of negative, disempowering thoughts, you have the ability to change the thought playlist in a matter of seconds. Start by asking: What is this situation trying to teach me? What can I be grateful for in this moment? How can I become a bigger version of myself with the help of these circumstances? Everything, including the challenging times, happens to help us become better people.

What are you choosing to focus on now? Are you stuck in a sad and frustrating loop, where you feel powerless? Or are you taking an empowered position, where you are choosing to learn the valuable lessons from every single one of your experiences?

When we find ourselves in traumatic situations, it is important to create positive experiences for ourselves at the same time. This is known as self-care. Self-care is actions that are designed to make us feel good; they can also be linked with our interests and our passions. It can be as simple as connecting with a loved one over the phone, taking a hot bath, going for a walk in nature, or developing a new hobby. Arlene shares a few different ways that helped her cope with her experiences. She began writing poetry and short stories; she also opened up and shared her experiences with others. Arlene understood that these activities would help her cope, and to accept what happened to her in a positive manner. Igniting passion in her life helped her to focus on herself rather than letting the difficult circumstances control her. Remember her very wise words: "Finding an outlet was great for two reasons: It gave me purpose, something I could do, something I enjoyed doing. And it gave me a way to express myself, a way to process my emotions, which in turn enabled me to let go of them and move on. Finding my passion was freeing and therapeutic; it gave me direction when I had never felt so lost."

How do you feel about what Arlene wrote? What can you do for yourself that would ignite your passion and help you cope with a challenging situation?

# Chapter 3

## Becoming a Kid of ACTION
by Kate McCobb

*"We do not need magic to transform our world.
We carry all the power we need
inside ourselves already."*
~J.K. Rowling~

**Iris:** When you are facing a challenge or trying out a new activity, confidence is *really* important! It gives you the courage to do all the amazing things you dream of doing in your life! Sometimes, as you will see in Kate's story, having confidence means getting out of your own way; it means getting out of your own head. When we are thinking about trying something new, fear wants to take over and protect us. We start over-thinking, and then we're stuck in *analysis-paralysis*. We're so busy trying to figure out what might happen if we take the next step that we forget to take the next step! *Always* have confidence, and trust in yourself, and good things will happen. Need help with a challenging situation? Just be confident!

Being confident means that you know you'll find the answers; it means you trust yourself and that you've got your own back, no matter what comes next. Never forget: YOU CAN DO IT!

**"Never regret a day in your life.**
**Bad days give you experience;**
**good days give you happiness."**
**~unknown~**

* * *

*Hello, my name is Kate. One day in school, our teacher introduced us to the concept of student council. I'd heard of it before, but I wasn't too interested. Our teacher talked really enthusiastically, and it seemed like our school was really a big part of it. She asked if any of us wanted to participate. I felt nervous inside, and I didn't know what to expect. I really didn't have much time to decide—only one student from each homeroom gets chosen, and we were just about to nominate! What was I going to do?*

*When it comes to making decisions like these, having confidence is really important. Sometimes you have to take a risk and **just do it!** My Auntie Jennifer is a really amazing role model for me when it comes to listening to your heart and having the courage to follow your dreams. Auntie was at the finish line* *during the Boston Marathon bombing. One of the ways that she chose to recover from the experience was to run the marathon herself, in 2017. When she made the decision, the marathon was only 5 1/2 months away. There were people, including her trainer, who told her that there wasn't enough time to prepare for the race in her condition. They told her to wait another year. But my Auntie knew, deep in her heart, that this was the year to heal from her trauma. She didn't give up. Auntie had an amazing circle of friends and practitioners who believed in her. Whenever she started doubting herself—and she did, many times during her training—they encouraged her to keep going. And guess what? Not only did she run the marathon, but she finished it even stronger!*

*If I had thought too much about my decision to run for student council, I would have probably stopped myself. Like my Auntie, I decided to follow my heart and the little voice that was whispering deep inside of me. I reminded myself that I was actually looking for a new activity. I decided to just take the chance and go for it! I was nominated as a candidate, and another person seconded the motion. The next thing I knew, I was in the running, and the vote was the next day!*

*This is the message I sent to my classmates before the vote:*

Hi, classmates; I'm running for student council, and I really would love your vote! If you have ideas, let me know, and I will talk to the student council about making it happen. I will definitely represent our class, and I think I can make this school great! I would really appreciate you voting for me. Vote from your heart, and not for who all your friends vote for.

WANT THINGS GREAT? VOTE FOR KATE!

*My teacher wasn't going to tell us the winner until our next project block, two days later. But the Google Form gave her the winner right away, and she decided to tell us. The winner was Kate McCobb! I was so happy! I finally found an activity I was meant for.*

\* \* \*

**Iris:** Do you know that everything is energy, including your thoughts and words? How do you talk to yourself? Do you cheer yourself on and raise yourself up, or do you criticize yourself and bring yourself down? One way paves the way toward your dreams, while the other way creates frustration and negativity. Everything we need is already inside of us. You'll never find what you are looking for outside of yourself. Look at how Kate handled her decision to run for student council. She was supportive, uplifting, and encouraging toward herself. She was her own best cheerleader—that helped her make a positive decision for herself.

What happens when you encounter people who talk down to you? You can simply walk away from these people. Just remember that hurt people, hurt people. We may think it is about us, but usually, people are discouraging because they are jealous of us, and they want to lash out in hopes of making us feel bad. Nobody can make you feel bad unless you allow them. You will never be able to control others' behavior, but you can always control your response. Choose to be loving and kind. Never stoop to their level. And what happens when it's our own voice that is talking down to us? Time to change the channel! Focus on the positive—remind yourself what you are learning from the situation. Raise yourself up!

Another way to create a more positive mind-set is by saying your prayers. This is really important because you are telling God (or whichever High Power you believe in) about the intentions you have for your life. Sometimes it's about asking for help in a challenging situation; sometimes it's about asking for an exciting opportunity to come into your life. Saying our prayers is an activity that ought to be done every day! It doesn't have to be a set time, and I believe that right before bed is ideal. Think about it as a way of connecting to something that is bigger and more powerful than you. Praying helps you develop a sense of connection. You can just talk to God, or another family member that has passed away. Tell them about your day, and about what is making you feel grateful. Tell them about your dreams, and about the places where you need some help. Don't think it's silly! I encourage you to give it a try and see what happens!

# Chapter 4

# Challenges Make Me Stronger
by Marissa Gallego

*"Life's challenges aren't here to break you. Life's challenges are here to mold, refine, and make you into all you were intended to become."*
~Billy Cox~

**Iris:** There is no doubt that a parent's divorce has the potential to create a fair amount of trauma in an entire family's life. But did you know that despite it seeming like a negative and sad situation, it's also an incredible opportunity for growth and development? I know, I know. You are probably shaking your head and disagreeing with me. But it's the truth! There are two key ingredients that can take any situation and turn it from a disempowering set of circumstances to an empowering opportunity to expand and grow.

The first ingredient is gratitude. No matter what is going on in your life, find some aspect of the situation that you can be grateful for. The fight with your sister allows you to express yourself, and liberates you from some negative emotions that were weighing you down. That oral presentation might have you shaking in your boots, but you know it's an incredible opportunity to flex your bravery muscles and share your voice with your class. No matter the challenge, there are always positive aspects. Think of it as going on a treasure hunt. There might not seem like there's anything on the surface. You might have to dig deep to find that piece of gold, but boy, will you be rewarded!

Gratitude has the power to shift EVERYTHING in your life. It has the power to heal, it will shift your perspective, it will make your heart expand, and it will improve your relationships with those you love. Even though Marissa was saddened by her parent's divorce, she chose to take an attitude of gratitude and be aware of all the elements that were working positively in her life. As you read her story, see if you can list all the different ways that she is grateful.

Now, I mentioned that there were two ingredients to turning a traumatic event into an empowering opportunity. What's the second ingredient, you ask? Keep reading—I'll tell you at the end of Marissa's story!

\* \* \*

## The Beginning

At a very young age, my parents got divorced. I was around four, and my sister, Julia, was two. I can't remember much, but I do faintly remember the day that my parents moved apart from each other. I remember feeling confused and not exactly knowing what was going on. My dad told me that I was very happy and that I was upstairs in the bedroom with him. I was dancing to what had been my favorite song, while my mom was outside with the moving truck men. I didn't really think much of it at first, and it wasn't until about three weeks later that I realized my sister and I hadn't seen my father for a while, and I remember missing him a lot. We got to see him when he was temporarily living in this little place in Rhode Island; it was right on the water, and I would feed the ducks bread. That was one of the only things I remember about going there. After that, he found a girlfriend named Tammy! We would visit her apartment often. It didn't really bother me because I still got to see my parents. Tammy was really nice, and she instantly became a huge part of my life. Although I can't recall being too upset about my parents' divorce, I would feel sad when I looked back at old photos of us all together—I still sometimes feel sad. If your parents are going through a divorce, please remember that you are not alone. It will get better—I promise!

## My Relationships

*Even though my parents are divorced, they still get along really well; that makes it much easier for me to have a good relationship with both of them. I have a really great relationship with my mom; I can tell her anything, and we get along really well! My dad and I have the same type of relationship too. I do live with my mom more, because she lives near where I go to school and also where I dance, and it makes it much easier. I do get to see my dad every other weekend though. It would be hard to be with him on school nights because I would have to get up really early to get to school. I'm just so happy that I still get along really well with both of them!*

## Look on the Bright Side

*When you are dealing with a challenging situation, like your parents' divorce for example, it's important to remember that there is always going to be a light at the end of the tunnel. It might not come right away, but it will come eventually. It may seem like the worst time in your life, but things will shift, and you will start to feel differently. Never forget this!*

*For my sister, my dad, and me, things really shifted when Tammy came into our lives. I remember going to her apartment a lot—we even went over there on*

*Christmas Day. Slowly but surely, we started to get closer to Tammy, and we met her whole family. They are all so loving; it is easy to be around them and talk to them. Tammy and my dad have been together now for 8 years, and she treats Julia and me as if we were her own kids. I've also become really close to Tammy's family, especially her daughter, and her daughter's husband, as well as Tammy's mom. I'm so happy for my dad and for my sister and me, because I couldn't imagine life without Tammy and her family. As for my mom, she started dating a man named Barry. I am just starting to get to know him—we do a lot of stuff with Barry, including going to beaches and just hanging out. Barry has two kids, named Jack and Quinn. Even though they are a little bit older than my sister and me, they are still fun to hang out with. We usually play neighborhood tag, or fortnight, which is always fun. I still do get sad sometimes when I see my friends with their whole families together, but if my parents hadn't gotten divorced, I would never have met all the amazing people that are now a part of my life!*

\* \* \*

**Iris:** Marissa could have been devastated by her circumstances, and she could have decided to give the events that were occurring in her life more power than how she interpreted and acted toward them.

Instead, she used that second ingredient that I mentioned, to transform her experience. What is that ingredient? It is the power of choice. Marissa chose to see the good that was coming from the divorce; she chose to believe that there was a light at the end of the tunnel. And even when she is sad about what she no longer has, she makes a conscious choice to focus upon all the love that is available to her.

Choice is a very powerful ingredient in your life. It puts you in the driver's seat and lets you create the life that you truly desire. Think about the following scenario: Two friends are excited to spend the day together. They each come with a list, with all sorts of different things that they could do. In the worst scenario, known as the *lose-lose* scenario, friends have nothing in common on their lists, and they simply cancel their day together and leave feeling very disappointed. In the *win-lose* scenario, one friend needs to make a compromise in order to spend time together—she loves that they're together, but she ends up doing an activity that she doesn't really enjoy. In the *win-win* scenario, the friends come together and choose to create an activity that works for both of them. Through the power of choice, they create an experience that is uniquely their own.

You are always just one choice away from creating a more positive outcome for yourself. Choice allows you to find your voice; it helps you to speak up for yourself and define what is most important for you. Remember to always look for the good in what is happening to you. Remember to be grateful, and remember that no matter what is happening in your life, you always have a say in how you are going to react and deal with life's events. You always get to choose how you will live your life.

# Chapter 5

# Staying Strong
by Raven Reitano

*"Always believe that something
wonderful is about to happen."*
~Dr. Sukhraj Dhillon~

**Iris:** One of the most challenging things we have to do in our lives is to ask for the things that we need. It would be so much easier if people could just read our minds and anticipate our needs without us having to say a word! But that is not how it works. It is vitally important to speak up for yourself.

Don't be scared to ask someone for something, especially when you trust them. Sometimes it means asking for support when you don't want to face an event alone. Sometimes it means asking for help to find solutions to a challenge that has been causing stress in your life. There is no doubt that asking for help can make you feel vulnerable, and have you thinking..."What if they say no?" What if they don't take your request seriously? What if they laugh?

*41*

Remember, you can't predict what will happen, and "what if's" will always keep you procrastinating asking for what you need and want out of life If you do not ask, then the answer will always be no. Muster up the courage to speak up and ask for what you need.

There is a part of Raven's story that focuses upon asking for help. As you read, see if you can put yourself in Raven's shoes, and then put yourself in her best friend's shoes. How would you have reacted to the situation? What would you have done?

\* \* \*

### *Bravery Cannot Come Without Fear*

*You meet someone new and start a conversation. "Do you have any siblings?" is a question that often comes up. I sometimes get stumped on how to answer. If I say I'm an only child, that line of conversation stops, and I don't need to worry about sharing my story. Sometimes, when I don't want to see the pity in their eyes, it's the best answer I can give.*

**"Everyone's background is different. It's up to you to make your life a good one."**
**~Raven Reitano~**

*But the truth is that I do have a sister, and this is our story. My sister's name is Athena Noelle. When she was little, she enjoyed Elmo, red M&Ms, and playing dolls with me. Sadly, I don't have too many of these memories. When she was three, Athena's head started to droop to the side, and she couldn't lift it back up. This is when the doctors realized that she had an incurable disease called metachromatic leukodystrophy; also known as MLD. To explain this in simpler terms, imagine a phone charger. It has a rubber coating on the outside to protect the wires from being exposed. The human body works the same way. We have nerves that are protected by a substance called myelin. This wraps around our nerves, creating a protective layer, just like the rubber protecting the wires on a phone charger. Nerves are what gives the body our senses. My sister's nerves no longer had their protective layer. This made her body unable to function properly. She was unable to move or speak—to me, she looked like a porcelain doll.*

**"Everyone has a choice to take their experiences and make good memories or bad ones. Bad things happen, but you can use these experience to find good."**
**~Raven Reitano~"**

*Life is very different when you have a sick sister. I was no longer able to play with her. My family had to be in and out of the hospital all the time, and we also constantly had nurses at our house. I could still read books and watch movies and television with my sister. I remember that her favorite show was Peep in the Big Wide World. She could no longer eat like a normal kid. Instead, twice a day, she had a machine to pump what looked like a vanilla milkshake into her stomach. Occasionally, she was able to lick a lollipop or eat a little bit of frosting from a birthday cake.*

## Unleash the Power Within You

*My family is an average family. My mom was a stay-at-home mom, and my dad worked on cars. At the time, the disease was unknown, and doctors did the best they could. We spent a lot of time and effort fundraising for non-profit organizations so that research could go into the disease. Our main focus was collecting can tabs. The price was determined by the pound, and strangers from near and far would send us buckets and buckets of can tabs to help us raise money. My school's cafeteria also had a corner for collecting can tabs.*

**"Go out of your comfort zone and experience helping someone in need."**
**~Raven Reitano~**

*We also had an annual bike race. Luckily, we lived on the same street as a small amusement park. Since they were only ever open for the winter season, they allowed us to host the bike ride for Athena there. The shortest distance was always a ten-mile course, which my friends and I would participate in. You could also choose either a 25-mile or 50-mile course. I always thought it was neat to see the tents set up for people who worked hard to make this race happen. Many wonderful people came together to help my family. Relatives, friends, and strangers helped raise the money that, in turn, helped my sister survive. If you ever get the opportunity, participate in a fundraiser to help those in need.*

**Surround Yourself with Positive People**

*The nurses that helped my sister also played a large part in our lives. When they were on duty, they practically lived at my house, and when my parents needed a break, they would also keep an eye on me. I'd like to thank Denise, Lynne, Jen, Stephano, Auntie Janeen, and Auntie Lori for hanging with me while still doing your job of taking care of my sister. Lynne was the youngest of the nurses, and that's probably why I got along with her the best.*

**"You never know who your friends will be, they come in all shapes and sizes. But when you find a good one, let them know."**
**~Raven Reitano~**

*We enjoyed the same television shows, such as Family Feud, and any home makeover show that was on. She would talk to me as a person and not as a little girl. Then the day came when she announced that she was moving across the country. I was super sad. Lynne and my mom went off one day and came back with a little gray kitten, and handed her to me. I decided I wanted Lynne to name her. She named the kitten Holi, short for holiday, because it was nearing Christmas. Holi became a part of our family and is still a major part of my life. She sleeps with me at night, and unlike most cats, loves to be held and will grab as much attention as she possibly can.*

### You Have to Be Strong in Tough Times

*My family always held on to hope. We had hope that a cure would be found, and that my sister would be healthy again. Sometimes what you wish for goes in the complete opposite direction. It was July 7th.*

**Stepping in to help someone may be temporarily painful to you, but could literally save another person's life!**

*I was eleven years old, and my sister was going to be turning nine in a month. My best friend was having a sleepover at my house. Early in the morning, my mom barged into my room. We woke up, and I could see tears streaming down my mother's face. And suddenly, everything felt like it was happening in slow motion. My mom told us that my sister's heart had stopped beating and that an ambulance was on its way.*

**Don't be afraid to ask your friends for help, and don't be afraid to help your friends. Helping one another creates a closer bond in which you know someone has your back.**

*My parents both went to the hospital, and we had to wait at the house until my grandparents picked us up. I remember sitting quietly at my grandparents' house for a few hours. We probably had the television going for some noise. The phone finally rang. My grandpa took the call in the other room, came back, and then handed me the phone. It was my dad. His voice sounded scratchy because he was crying. I had never heard him cry before. I remember his words so clearly. "I'm sorry Rave, she didn't make it." I didn't cry; I just sat in stunned silence. My little sister had passed away. My grandparents tried to give me a pep talk, and my best friend didn't know what to say. Instead, she called her aunt to come and pick her up. When she left my grandparents' house, I felt very alone. I don't blame her in the least for leaving during this time. We were eleven, and it was news that no one wanted to hear. If I had any advice for friends that know someone with a family member that has recently passed, I would suggest you ask them if they want a shoulder to lean on. You can sit in silence or talk if they want to talk, but sometimes just having the presence of a friend is comforting. If they want to be alone, give them their space, but never assume that is what that person wants. If I could go back in time and give myself some advice, I would tell myself to be courageous and ask my friend to stay by my side. If I had uttered that request, I know she would have stayed with me. And for those who are facing a challenging situation themselves, please don't be afraid to ask for a supporting hand when you need one.*

### Stay Strong, Keep Smiling

*What came after my sister's death was a lot of preparation for the funeral. Every day, I would go with my family to visit my sister in the funeral home. I painted her nails and made sure she was dressed in pajamas, because I wanted her last outfit to be comfy.*

**"Colors speak louder than words... surround yourself with colors that make you happy."**
**~Raven Reitano~**

*Normally, there is a wake before a funeral. This is where friends and loved ones are able to say goodbye. I decided not to go; I didn't want others to see me cry. I didn't want endless people coming up to me and giving me their condolences. When it was over, my mom mentioned a few people that did attend. Their names brought a smile to my face. Former teachers came. Kids from school that I was simply friendly toward dropped by. People who I had not thought about in years also attended. I want to thank all of those people.*

*The next day was the funeral. My only request was that everyone should dress in colorful clothes. I thought the typical black attire that you see in films was too dreary. Funerals will always be sad, but when you are surrounded by colors that make you happy, it's easier to think of all the good times you were able to experience with the person who has died. I will also always appreciate what my mom did for me at the funeral. She made sure I had sunglasses to wear. It might seem odd for a funeral, but it allowed me to cry freely without worrying about everyone staring at me. It was a shield for me.*

*The funeral went by quietly, and soon after, my house was quiet—no more medical machines; no more nurses coming in and out of the house. I sat on my bed, next to my mom, and asked, "What are we going to do now?" Her response was, "I don't know." My family took things one step at a time. Even though I loved playing basketball, I ended up quitting my summer sports that year. My coach kept me in the loop on how the team was doing, and even sent me the medal at the end of the season. I have much gratitude for that. The next thing my family did was get a dog. He was a husky puppy named Nike, who was the Greek goddess Athena's best friend. He was a ball of energy that added a little noise back into our lives.*

*I'm not going to lie. For a while I felt empty and a little bitter at the world. I grew up having so much hope that life was going to become better for my sister. She would get better and be able to be a kid and go to school. Then, everything just ended; my sister was gone, and a cure was never found. It took me a while to overcome these feelings, and in some ways, I am still working them out.*

*In middle and high school, I decided that it was my duty to get an education that would lead me to a degree in biology, so that I could help find the cure for Athena's disease. Then I got to college. I was taking my second biology course, and I realized that I hated* it. I did not want my future career to be linked with something that I disliked. I don't think my sister would have liked me choosing a career that I disliked either. Currently, I am a graphic design major, and still in school. I am still growing up and figuring out my life. I have reached a point where I am okay to open up and share my sister's story. Not everything has to be taken in massive strides; sometimes it requires falling down and taking small steps forward. Always go at your own pace. I will always cherish the time I shared with my sister, even though it was short.

## When Life Brings You Down ... Stand up Strong

I think that my sister's endless visits to the doctors affected me and caused me to have a fear of doctors. When I was younger, I would become a real pain at my yearly check-up; and if I had to get a shot, I turned into a little monster—I was terrified of needles! Today, my fear of doctors is greatly reduced, but I had to overcome at lot.

**"Spend less time on thinking of what could have been. Instead smile at the memories, and create a path that leads to happiness."**
**~Raven Reitano~**

When my family thinks of my sister, we always associate her with an image of a dragonfly. When we *would have fundraisers, everyone would wear t-shirts with Athena's Hope written on them. The A in the name was created by putting two dragonflies together. Whenever we see a dragonfly, we always think of Athena. Soon after her death, many people, friends, and family who had been in her life, started getting tattoos of dragonflies, in memory of Athena. I had turned eighteen, and I still had a fear of needles. I really wanted to get a tattoo, but it took me a long time to decide. Finally, I drew a design myself, and made an appointment for the tattoo to be placed on my wrist. It's a fairly small tattoo, but now I am no longer afraid of needles. And whenever I have a doctor's appointment, I look at that dragonfly.*

*There is another group I have to mention that provided help to our family when we were in need. Bethany's Hope is an organization based in Canada that is looking for a cure for metachromatic leukodystrophy. They are currently raising money for clinical trials.*

*Families now have solid hope to grasp onto for their children suffering with this disease. When my sister was sick, not a lot was known about this illness. My mom happened to reach out to Bethany's family, who has a similar story to ours. Growing up, all my science projects in middle and high school were always about MLD, and Bethany's Hope was the organization I would look to for information. I can't wait for the day they announce that the first patient has been cured of this disease.*

**When Life Brings You Down... Stand Up Strong!**

\* \* \*

**Iris:** One of the keys to living a courageous life is to remember not to take things personally. If someone hasn't offered the help or support you need, it's not necessarily because they don't want to—it might be because they don't know how! When you are clear about what you need, it gives your loved ones an opportunity to rise up and meet those needs. Most people love to help. Speaking up allows you to create deeper bonds with those you love, enabling you to live authentically. Rather than putting on a brave face and pretending everything is fine, you are digging deep, being vulnerable, and showing people what's really going on in your life. This will help you move through challenging situations much more easily. Remember that you are never alone—there is always a hand to hold, so go ahead and reach for it.

Life can sometimes give us very challenging events to deal with, events that can make us sad, angry, or even frustrated. We fall into a trap when we believe that we cannot be happy until all those outside events are resolved. Believing this means we are taking away our power—we are at the mercy of what is happening outside of ourselves. On good days, we are happy; on bad days, we are sad. It's a rollercoaster, with no end in sight!

But did you know that there is a way to get off that ride? The key is to realize that happiness and wellbeing are inside jobs. Being happy is a journey— it's not a destination! When life gets tough, focus more on yourself: Focus on **FLYing** (**F**irst **L**ove **Y**ourself), focus on making healthy and empowering choices, remember your strengths, and ask for what you need. Remember to always come from the position of a victor. You are in charge of your life— how you react; your actions—these are all up to you! Of course, there are going to be times that you will feel sad, but by focusing on the lesson that you are being taught, rather than the events themselves, you will feel much, much happier and stronger!

# Chapter 6

# Cherishing Those We Love
by Julia Gallego

*"Grandparents bestow upon their grandchildren
the strength and wisdom that time and experience
have given them. Grandchildren bless their
grandparents with a youthful vitality and innocence
that helps them stay young at heart forever.
Together, they create a chain of love,
linking the past with the future.
The chain may lengthen but it will never part..."*
~unknown~

**Iris:** Challenging situations can sometimes leave us feeling in the dumps. We feel sad, we feel frustrated, and sometimes we get caught up in a negative cycle of thinking. "Why is this happening to me?" becomes the question that continually flashes in our brains. And that is not a helpful question! It puts you in the position of being a victim, and takes away your power. Instead, take a look at what the situation can teach you. What lesson is there to be learned? Are you learning to be more kind? More understanding?

Does this situation teach you about forgiveness, or how to be more loving toward yourself and others?

In Julia's story, she talks about learning to cope with watching her grandfather grow older. One tool she uses is the power of gratitude. You will notice that she focuses on all the happy memories that she has of him. Being thankful opens your heart; it casts out fear and brings you back into the present moment. In our lives, we have no control over the future; we only know that we have the present moment—and it is such a gift! Life can change in a second; the key is to live every single moment. That moment might be bringing you joy, or it might be teaching you a lesson—either way, be grateful for the opportunity you are being given! This attitude will lead you on the path toward a happier life.

\* \* \*

### Spending Quality Time with Grandpa

*My grandpa's name is Edward Gallego. He is a kind-hearted man, and I carry many fond memories of him from when I was younger. I cherish that he is still in my life today. Some of my best memories are from family dinners. We would all gather around the table and enjoy a delicious boiled dinner, which is made from different varieties of food, such as corn, cabbage, ham, and carrots, all mixed together into one large pot, with a side of biscuits (they were always my favorite!). After dinner, we all watched my grandpa's favorite TV shows—either cooking shows or Alligator Hunters. We sometimes spent the night, and he would treat us to popcorn, and two scoops of ice cream with whipped cream on top. Things are a little bit different now— around three years ago, my grandpa started getting sick.*

*When he first got sick, he had a serious infection. My grandpa was sent to the hospital for the infection, but they couldn't locate it. The doctors then sent him to the Boston Hospital for four days, until he was finally moved back to a nursing home rehab in Taunton. When he got back to the nursing home, they said he could now start the exercise class and physical therapy to build his strength back. About a week later, he went back to Boston for his first checkup. The infection was better but not gone, which meant he had to go back into rehab, where he would stay until his next check-up.*

*Personally, this was probably the hardest part for me. There was so much waiting and wondering! My grandpa had to stay in bed all day waiting for the medication to kick in. Then we were waiting for his check-up results, and he had to keep going back and forth from Taunton to Boston. I felt so helpless—the whole time I was sitting at home, worrying that something was going to happen to him.*

*My grandpa is 93, and at that age, you never know what is coming. I felt sad, and sometimes I would start to have negative thoughts. I tried my best to stay strong despite how I was feeling. One of the best ways of coping with negative thoughts is to engage in an activity that you enjoy—something that will focus your mind on something more positive. When I was five, it was very hard for me not to take my feelings out on other people, but now I know I have more self-control over my thoughts and my body. The other thing I do when I am upset is to take deep breaths to calm myself. Thinking positive thoughts can also clear your mind and bring you to your happy place. Try out some of these calming suggestions yourself, and see how they impact your life, your thoughts, your actions, and your feelings.*

*These coping skills helped me while my family waited to get the news about my grandpa. After about three and a half weeks in rehab, he was finally mobile again! He was soon able to go home and enjoy sleeping on his adjustable bed, and even start eating his two scoops of ice cream again! Even though my grandpa was doing much better, I was still a little sad, because I never got a chance to meet my Grandma May. My dad would always tell me that she was a beautiful woman, and that she got along really well with my grandpa—they got married in 1946! Grandma May died before I was born, but I think about her often, and I wish that we had been able to spend time together.*

*I know that it is hard to watch the people we love grow older. You are not alone in what you are feeling! I know it can be rough at times, but take a moment to realize how far our loved ones have come, and how much they have done with their lives. Remember that they've made it to the point where their systems are starting to slowly shut down. You don't know how much time is left—it could be days, weeks, or months. No matter what, make every day count, and make every moment the best!*

*Thank you Grandpa for being there throughout my life, and thank you Grandma for all that you gave to our family. I will always love both of you, and I will never forget you.*

**Grandparents are a magical blend of joy, laughter, wonderful stories, and unconditional love!**

\* \* \*

**Iris:** Did you know that you can feel two completely different emotions about the exact same set of circumstances? Julia could have chosen to feel sad, scared, and upset about her grandfather's illness. Instead, she chose to feel grateful, and to celebrate all the beautiful moments that they shared together. It is important to remember to tell the people in your life just how much you love them, and often, because you never know when they will go to Heaven.

Another key element in life is celebration. Celebration is essential for building momentum and continued success. When you take time to celebrate your accomplishments, even the little ones, it builds confidence and courage to keep moving forward, even when it gets more difficult. Celebration means looking at life as a gift, and focusing on all the details that are being used to create a more positive, happier life. An upbeat celebratory outlook creates a successful mindset and releases happy chemicals (serotonin and dopamine) into your body. These chemicals make you feel good, and the more you feel good about yourself, the stronger your energy becomes, and soon you are unstoppable.

# Chapter 7

## The Power of Letting Go
by Amanda Blake

*"The weak can never forgive.*
*Forgiveness is the attribute of the strong."*
~Gandhi~

**Iris:** There is no doubt that in order to lead a courageous life, you need to learn how to forgive and how to let go of events from your past. Lots of people mistakenly believe that forgiveness means that you are letting the people who hurt you off the hook. But that's not it at all! It's actually all about what happens to YOU in the process.

If you are unable to forgive, it means you are bringing all of those unresolved feelings into your present—which can be a pretty heavy weight to carry. An important part of forgiveness is being able to speak about your experience and how the events made you feel. Speak your feelings out loud—it can be to yourself or to a trusted friend—the key is to acknowledge the truth of your emotions. We've even got a special forgiveness process that you can use (found in chapter 11): Empowering YOU.

The next step is to let go of those emotions. If you attach yourself to what happened in your past, you will never have room in your present or your future for anything new! In the same way you clean your room and get rid of clothes and items that no longer serve you, you need to do the same thing with your feelings! Take a look at your inner world—what stories and emotions are you holding onto? What would it feel like if you let them go? What would you have room for in your life if these stories and emotions weren't there anymore?

Amanda's story is a powerful reminder that forgiveness is a process—it doesn't happen overnight—but if you stick with it, and remain committed to freeing yourself from your disappointments and hurt, you will see how much lighter and happier your life will become.

\* \* \*

### My Past Made Me Who I Am Today

*Accomplishing personal challenges can be intimidating. Feelings of defeat and loss can become suffocating; you begin believing that there is no way out. Turning those feelings around can be a lifelong journey. Mine began when I was five years old.*

*Throughout elementary school, I battled with the late night arguments between my parents, the emergency visits to the hospital with my younger brother, and the eventual separation of my parents. Around the age of ten, I had a new challenge: my parents' chaotic divorce. It involved restraining orders, regulated visiting hours with my father, as well as a new way of living that involved just my mom and younger brother. My father barely saw us.*

*After the divorce, from the time I was 10, until I was 14, I had to deal with my mother trying to find herself. She felt the need to be free, and she rebelled against everything. Her kind, nurturing self faded as she viewed herself as broken, and she was constantly looking for ways to fix herself. Random male friends frequently came over as she embarked upon a search for the partner that would make her feel whole. At the same time, I was looking for a father figure to replace my own father—someone who fit my ideal version of what a father should be—but no one stayed.*

*Throughout my late teenage years, from 14 to 19, I was faced with an even bigger change. My grandparents discovered what was going on in my home. From that point, my anxiety really started to show itself. I was struggling with the idea of my grandparents taking control, because I knew that wasn't what my mother wanted. If I sided with my grandparents, I felt that I would be disrespecting my mother's wishes. She wanted to handle everything on her own, when deep down, she needed help. I became so anxious at times, and I felt really depressed and couldn't sleep because, internally, I felt this was all my fault. My brother and I ended up moving into our grandparents' house. During this period, I had to relearn how to act like a child. I had to let go of feeling the need to be a mom toward my little brother, and I had to learn that it was okay to make mistakes and learn from them. The truth is, I was still struggling with letting go of how my parents behaved. I had expectations of who I wanted them to be.*

*Recently, I have embarked on a journey of healing. Going on this journey, I realized that healing is a lifelong journey that will have a beneficial impact upon my future, enabling me to have the healthy family I desire, and to work at my dream career.*

### Process of Healing

**"I'm strong; I'm incredibly strong.**
**I will become even stronger as I find my voice."**
**~Amanda Blake~**

*I'd like to talk to you about ways of healing. The process is ongoing, and it's not always easy! It takes time, patience, and determination. In the beginning, I thought the idea of forgiveness was insane. Until I learned the three key points to the process:*

1. *It's all about you, not forgiving the other person but accepting who they are.*
2. *It's important to embrace your raw emotions in a safe way.*
3. *It's essential to find someone you trust so that you can share those emotions.*

*The first point is the most important. In the beginning, I believed forgiveness meant that I had to forgive my parents for what they did to me, and move on. But that's not the case! This entire process is actually a way for me to connect with my raw emotions and let them out in a healthy way. I found writing down pages and pages about how I was feeling really helped me connect. I felt anger; I felt sadness and hurt, but I was able to process it in a healthy way that did not cause harm to me or anyone else. By going through this process, I was able to also reconnect with a therapist. By finding my way through healing, I was able to build a stronger support system that benefited me.*

*The key point is healing yourself. Recognizing that you need the time to step back and breathe, while evaluating your scenario, is part of self-care. Be patient with yourself; it takes time. Be kind to yourself, realizing that this is a big step in the right direction. In the end, it all depends on how you decide to control your process of healing. Really think about what advice you would give to someone else—and then follow that advice!*

*By going through this process of healing, I have been able to achieve a healthier mindset, and realize that I don't need to have toxic people in my life.*

### Accepting What Is...

**"As I get older, the more I stay focused on the acceptance of myself and others, and choose compassion over judgment, and curiosity over fear."**
**~Tracee Ellis Ross~**

*On my journey, I also had to learn about accepting my parents for who they are. Honestly, I don't fully accept them for who they are. It's hard, and that's okay. In the process of accepting my parents, I have learned to confide in those that I trust. For instance, I trust the support and perspective that my therapist provides when I am sad or don't know how to approach a specific scenario. Talking about my feelings and the expectations I had of both parents, helped me begin to accept them for who they are.*

*I am still learning that I can't change who they are. I never will be able to. However, knowing this can help me come to terms with who they are now. This, in turn, helps me be less disappointed when they make mistakes or don't meet my expectations. I am able to appreciate the trials I experienced with my parents, and to see how I was able to grow through those challenges. Though they may have hurt me and disappointed me, they helped me become who I am today. I wouldn't have the opportunities that I have now if I didn't go through what I did. Within every dark past, there is a door that opens to a brighter future.*

## Letting Go

**"Forgiveness allows you to free yourself from the shackles of your past."**
**~Amanda Blake~**

*Letting go is still a lesson I am learning. I used to feel that letting go was the same thing as forgiving someone. I let go, and it means that I was okay with everything that happened, even if I don't feel okay. This process, like the others mentioned above, is a life process. It has its moments that will make you question everything, but don't. You are stronger than you believe you are. Letting go, for me, wasn't about allowing my past to win; it was about allowing this weight I was carrying around to dissolve. I will never forget my past, yet I won't let it hold me back from what the world and God has to offer me. Moving on from my past will allow me to create a positive, healthier future. You can do the same. Allow yourself to really connect with your deep emotions and thoughts; write down what is bothering you, and read aloud what you wrote. Allow your emotions to flow in a safe way, and connect with what you are feeling. Holding back will create this extra weight that you don't need. Think of it as trying to get healthy enough to run a marathon. You may need to lose a little weight to move forward in running that marathon. In the process, you need to take action in getting there—no one else can do it for you. Crossing the finish line in a marathon is similar to letting go of the extra emotional weight, to benefit your future.*

*The truth is, deep down, I love my parents. I always wanted to please them and keep the peace in the family. However, I wasn't pleasing myself. It took me time to realize that with my parents, I need to know healthy boundaries to keep me happy. Right now, this includes disappointing my parents by not seeing them as much as they might want me to. I know I am able* to move on, and forgive, but I know, to keep me happy and healthy, I might also be disappointing them at the same time. *Learning to let go of the idea that people might get upset with my choices has been hard, but it is what kept me healthy and happy throughout the process.*

### Blessings in Life

*I encourage you to find the simple blessings in life. They can come in many shapes and sizes. Finding the blessings in life helps you to build a positive mindset, and leaves you feeling stronger and as if you can handle anything—which you can!*

*My simple blessings include living with my grandparents and having a unique younger brother. At times, it is hard. Truthfully, it can be hard being raised by grandparents, due to the generation gap. Generation gaps create misunderstandings, but they also allow for a learning experience on both sides. It also creates patience and respect for those who are older than you. At the age of 19, I realized they didn't need to help my brother and me the way that they did. We could have easily gone to foster care, but they wanted what was best for us. They gave me the hope that I needed, when I couldn't find it for myself. My grandparents turned out to be the parent role models I was searching for as a young child. I was given so many opportunities because of them. I have them to thank for guiding me down the right path and allowing me to grow, and for helping me to learn how to control my anxiety and to seek the help that I needed.*

*Having a brother who is so unique has taught me so many life lessons as well. My brother has FG syndrome and depression, as well as being borderline autistic and borderline bipolar. He has also had two heart surgeries and has dealt with multiple seizures. He is such a huge role model in my life. He has grown from someone who couldn't handle his emotions and was judged and picked on, to someone who is mentally stronger and kind hearted. He has grown with me through my journey, and has taught me so much about patience and accepting people for their quirks and disabilities. He is someone who I will forever have by my side—I know we will be able to cherish our accomplishments together.*

*I'm starting to recognize that my parents are also a blessing in my life; I wouldn't be here today if it wasn't for them. I also wouldn't be able to share my story, and help others, without knowing the pain I have been through. Through these events, I grew into the person I am today, and that is the greatest gift of all!*

*My hope and desire for you is that you never feel alone. Inner strength and motivation are the greatest tools to overcoming personal challenges. In the beginning of my process, it wasn't easy. At times, I did feel alone, but once I decided to open up to people I trusted, I was finally able to see the value and importance of expressing my feelings to others. My hope is that you are able to take that courageous step in healing.*

\* \* \*

**Iris:** Forgiveness becomes much easier when we are able to let go of our expectations and accept a situation for exactly what it is. Let's imagine that you were really excited about a picnic that was coming up on the weekend. You're picturing yourself riding your bike with your friends, and eating your favorite foods with your family, on a beautiful, sunny, warm day. But when you wake up on Saturday morning, it's pouring, and your plans have been cancelled. Getting upset at the situation is only going to make you feel worse—you can't control the weather! Your job is to accept what has happened, let go of your expectations, and do your best with what you've been given. Maybe you could go to a movie instead, or stay under the covers and read in bed all day!

The same is true when you are looking at disappointments in your life. Rather than get caught up in your expectations of what should have happened (that will only lead to more upset and frustration), you need to look inside and see how you can make yourself feel better right now. In the end, it's not about what's happening in the outside world—you can't control events or other people! It's about taking care of yourself, and trading your sadness and hurt for inner peace and wisdom. You'll end up with more love and joy within yourself, and soon you'll be seeing it in the outside world too!

# Chapter 8

# Say Goodbye to Your Comfort Zone
by Meghan McCobb

*"Once you break through your comfort zone,
your confidence will soar."*
~Meghan McCobb~

**Iris:** How do you feel when I mention the word, *failure*? Is it a negative word that makes you want to run in the other direction? Are you so scared of making a mistake, and do you stop yourself from going outside of your comfort zone? Do you judge yourself, and believe that failure means you are not good enough? Life is about learning, growing, and failures! The word, *FAIL*, simply means **F**irst **A**ttempt **I**n **L**earning. Don't be afraid to fail; be afraid of not trying. Learning from your mistakes allows you to become a better person; it allows you to make a better life for yourself! Maybe not in the way you had necessarily planned, but you will learn something new from your experiences. Succeeding or failing really isn't the point—the key is to pick yourself up and keep moving forward. Keep stepping outside of your comfort zone and discovering new things: about the world around you and about yourself. Become curious about life, and never give up. Throughout her life, Meghan has always been willing to try new things. Read about her experiences, and get ready to be inspired!

* * *

### Recognize Your Progress: PMC Heavy Hitter Challenge

*At the age of four, I started to learn about goal setting and the importance of giving back. My parents signed me up to participate in a bike ride fundraiser called the PMC Kids Ride (a.k.a. PMC Heavy Hitter Breakaway Fundraiser). I was a rider who raised enough money to reach the level of fundraising where I had a direct link to a kid who had been affected by cancer.*

**"The more you celebrate your life,
the more there is in life to celebrate."
~Oprah Winfrey~**

*In other words, I had the opportunity to raise money, with the help of my family, for the Dana-Farber Cancer Institute, which cares for patients, and finds new ways to cure cancer. Over the next three years, I* *participated in this fundraiser. Each year, I raised over $300, and I was honored as a PMC Heavy Hitter. My sister, Kate, and I were two of the many kids who were very courageous to ride for a good cause, and we learned not to be afraid to ask people for donations. Every year, my sister and I did this race, and we had a blast! We loved bike riding, and it was way better when we knew it was for a great cause.*

*After doing laps around a neighborhood in our town, we were always super excited to go into the school and see if we were a Heavy Hitter. We were excited not only to be honored, but to know that just the few hundred dollars we raised could help find a cure for a life threatening disease.*

*Every year, we were called up and were rewarded with a medal. When we got that medal, we definitely knew that we had made a difference in someone's life, just by raising a little money.*

*Being courageous and doing this challenge was definitely a life changing moment for us, and for the unfortunate people in the hospital!*

*Here are a few things that I learned from the challenge, when it comes to achieving your goals:*

## 1. Identify your goals
   *a. Example: PMC Heavy Hitter Challenge*

   *b. There are several options for participating in this particular challenge, which include:*

      *i.  Each motivated rider, who raises $300 or more, will be honored as a PMC Kids Heavy Hitter.*

      *ii.  Those who raise $800 or more will be honored as a PMC Kids Breakaway Fundraiser.*

   *c. Choose the goal best for you, and make sure it stretches you outside your comfort zone.*

## 2. Break it down
   *a. Make a list of family and friends who can contribute to help you reach your goal(s).*

   *b. Ask family or friends if they will ask others to contribute.*

   *c. Fundraise at events in your town/ school.*

   *d. Create your own fundraiser (sell lemonade, sell friendship bracelets, mow lawns, have a yard sale, babysit).*

## 3. Take ACTION

## 4. Celebrate your progress
   *a. It is important to celebrate even your smallest progress in order to keep moving forward.*

b. *Ways to celebrate*
   i.    *Record it in your success journal*
   ii.   *Tell someone*
   iii.  *Jump up and down*
   iv.  *Treat yourself to a reward*
   v.   *Positive self-talk*

*NOTE: Repeat this process until you reach your goal.*

### I Am Brave Enough to Try: My Thunder Mountain Experience (Age 8)

*A couple of years ago, my family and I went to Disney World, in Florida. I was super excited for all the rides, but I was most nervous for the Thunder Mountain ride. I knew it would be fun, but I also knew it was a roller coaster that went very fast and had very twisty turns. I was scared!*

*As I walked into Disney World, I was filled with so much excitement! Everywhere I looked, there were so many rides and so many kids! We went on a bunch of rides, and then it was time to go on Thunder Mountain. We were fortunate that we did not have to wait too long, because we were in the fast pass line. Soon, it was our turn to get on the ride, and my heart was pounding as if I had just ran a marathon.*

*I wanted to ride with my dad, so we walked to the back of the roller coaster and sat in one of the back seats. My heart was pounding so fast, and I felt a series of chills run down my spine. All of a sudden, the ride started, and I said to myself, "There is no getting off now!" We slowly went up a very steep hill,*

*and as soon as we got to the top, I panicked. I think most people know that once you go up, you somehow have to get back down. My heart dropped, and all I heard were the screams of other children and their families on the ride. Once we got down the big hill, I felt a little better and started to accept the ride. Slowly, all of the chills went away, and my heart calmed down. By the end of the ride, I felt like I could conquer anything. I was very glad that I had gone on that ride, and I wasn't scared of any other ride to come.*

**"All our dreams can come true...**
**if we have the courage to pursue them."**
**~Walt Disney~**

### Reaching for New Heights (Age 9)

*Two years ago, my Auntie Jennifer invited my family and me to a private fundraising event, where Kristen Merlin, a singer in the top five on season number 6 of The Voice, was singing. My aunt asked me if I wanted to sing with her, should an opportunity come up. Although I definitely wanted to do it, I wasn't sure whether or not I could do it.*

*When Kristen Merlin was setting up, my family and I went over and started talking to her. We got pictures,* and she gave us glow sticks. Kristen also gave us autographed posters of herself. Soon, she started singing—she has a beautiful voice.

During a break, my aunt and I went over and asked Kristen if it was possible for me to sing with her. I felt very nervous as we approached her, because I had never sang with a real singer before, and I didn't know what her answer was going to be. She said I could sing with her, but I would have to wait a while until she was done with all her songs.

Then, the "Cotton-Eyed Joe" song came on, and she came down and danced with all the people at the small fundraiser. When that was done, Kristen and some other people started setting up for what I thought was going to be me going onstage. I started to feel a little nervous but excited at the same time.

They finished setting up and, right then, I realized that it was another singer performing. Now I had to wait another hour until they finished singing. Once they were done, Kristen finished up with a couple of songs, and she started to set up another microphone for me. I was very excited and also a little nervous. She called me up on stage, and I can't even remember walking up there. She asked me my name, and I told her it was Meghan. Everyone started chanting my name. She asked me what song I wanted to sing. At first, I didn't *know, and then I decided to go with a Taylor Swift song, "Blank Space." I knew the words well, and I was comfortable singing it.*

*The music started to play, and I couldn't believe I was actually singing. When we finished the song, I walked off stage, and everyone started chanting my name again.*

*Kristen Merlin finished up the night singing one last song, and we got in our car and drove home. Even though it was a late night, it was by far one of the most fun nights I've ever had!*

**"I am going to hit the ground running."**
**~Kristen Merlin~**

### Take a Risk and Go for It (Age 11)

*Our school went on a field trip to the YMCA sports complex, and my grade signed up to do the ropes course. When we got there, many people thought the ropes course looked sketchy and not very safe. I didn't really know what to think; I knew the staff wouldn't let us on if it wasn't safe, but it did look dangerous. There were two trees and a thick wire leading from one tree to the other, with 4 ropes hanging about 5 feet apart from each other.*

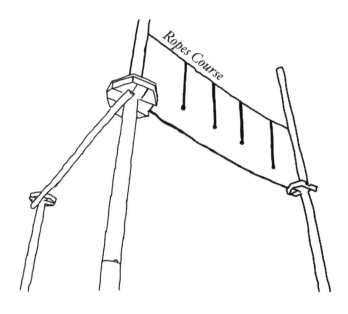

*As I kept looking up at the rope course, I noticed people coming down before climbing all the way up to the wire to walk across. It was my turn, and all of a sudden, a nervous feeling swept all over my body. The people who had climbed part of the way up said that the wire was much higher than they thought, and that it was even scarier from up above the ground. As I got into my harness, I began to shake all over. There was one person up on the wire, and two of us on the ground, harnessed and waiting to go. The person in front of me ended up chickening out at the last second, and made me go first.*

**"Even though some people may say it is scary you won't know until you give it a try..."**
**~Meghan McCobb~**

*My body wasn't prepared at all, and suddenly, I found myself getting hooked onto the pulley system. I managed to get myself together, and I started climbing up the ladder that led to the staples hooked into the tree, just below the wire. I got to the wire and put one foot down. It was shaking without me even putting my full weight on it. I started thinking about how shaky it would be when I put my full weight on it. I stepped on the wire, and I was definitely stepping outside of my comfort zone. I made it to the first rope that was hanging down vertically. I took a few more steps and, magically, I was halfway across the wire, holding on to the second rope. When I made it to the third rope, I knew that I was not turning back, and I was determined to finish, no matter how hard it was! With that attitude, I made it to the fourth rope! Now it was time to jump backwards off the wire, where most of the other kids had the hardest time building up the confidence. 1...2...3... I counted in my head, and down I went. I was very proud of myself for conquering my fears and going outside of my comfort zone. The rest of the field trip turned out to be amazing.*

**Have the courage to do the scary things in life...it's how you will grow!**

## Listen to the Voice Inside You: A Story About my Grandmother, Nan (Age 11)

*Last April, my grandmother, Nan, passed away due to cancer. When it came time for my dad and his three siblings to plan the wake and funeral, there was an opportunity for my cousin and me to serve at the altar during her funeral. We both have experience in altar serving. It was a tough and nerve-racking decision, but my cousin and I agreed to do it because we both knew that was what our grandmother would have wanted.*

*When that day came, I was very nervous and sad. The saddest part was when our close family came together and said our last goodbyes. Even though I was scared, I knew that I was doing the right thing. On the way to the funeral, many thoughts came into my head. I knew that my cousin was very nervous as well, because we had never served at that church before. I also knew that even though my grandmother wasn't there in person, I felt she would be there looking over me.*

*We got to the church, and my cousin and I put on our robes, and the priest walked us through the things we needed to do. I felt a bit more comfortable, but I was still very nervous.*

*Since we got there earlier than everyone else, we waited in a small hallway until the mass started. Waiting in that hallway was one of the worst parts— I got very nervous. The ceremony started, and all of my nerves went away. I finally had enough courage to go out there and make my grandmother proud!*

*When the funeral ended, I was pleased with what my cousin and I had accomplished. I knew that it wasn't only my grandmother who would have been proud of us; I think our friends and family were proud too. Making that decision was a great choice for me because it took a lot of courage to overcome my fears and just do it!*

**"If you really believe in yourself, listen to your inner voice, and do what you love; you will always succeed."**
**~Meghan McCobb~**

### *Visualize Success: Basketball Story (Age 12)*

*Right in the middle of last basketball season, I buckle fractured my right wrist. Basketball means a lot to me, especially in the winter months. It was dreadful for me to miss out on playing a sport I love. That year, I had tried out for both my school team and my town team, and I ended up making both teams. I worked very hard to make those teams, and my participation meant a lot to me; it was horrible when I was told I couldn't play. The doctors initially told me that I would not be able to play for the rest of the season.*

*I was in a cast for three weeks before going back to my doctor for a checkup. When they removed my cast to do another x-ray, I was so nervous; I had no idea what the doctor would say. Surprisingly, my arm was healing faster than planned, and I could wear a brace for the next two weeks as it continued to heal. I was so excited because it gave me hope that I might be able to play basketball again, before the end of the season.*

*During those two weeks, all I could think about was being able to play in my last basketball game of the season. My Auntie Jennifer had taught me about the power of visualizations and affirmations. I spent each day picturing my wrist fully healed. I saw myself playing basketball and enjoying time with my teammates on the court. I used as many senses as I could during my visualization, to give my body the full experience of having a healed wrist. I could hear my teammates cheering aloud: "Go Meghan go!" I could feel my hand on the ball while preparing for my shot. Doing this visualization actually got me excited! I kept telling myself, "I can do this!" while imagining and feeling what it would be like to return to the basketball court before the end of the season. Each time that I was doubtful during my recovery—and trust me, I was—I would simply stop myself and return to imagining and feeling what it would be like to play again. Rather than feeling down and depressed, which is an option, I chose to focus on raising my vibration until I felt inspired, enthusiastic, and hopeful. I learned that the more I raised my vibration with my thoughts and imagination of the outcome I wanted, the more my energy increased. When we focus on uplifting feelings, it releases happy chemicals in our body, which can accelerate the healing process. If I can do it, so can you!*

*My follow-up appointment to get another x-ray was just two days before my last game. I thought about how amazing it would be to be able to play one last game. I did everything to make sure I could play in that game, but I didn't know if any of it would work.*

*I went to my doctor for my follow-up appointment, and I was very scared to walk into the x-ray room. I was nervous because I knew it would go one of two ways:*

*1. I get to play, or*
*2. My wrist still isn't strong enough*

*I patiently waited in a room and, finally, they came in and told me the results. My arm was healed, and I HAD A CHANCE TO PLAY! I had to strengthen my wrist in the next day to be sure that it was strong enough to play.*

**The moment you're ready to quit is usually the moment right before the miracle happens. NEVER GIVE UP!**

*I did everything I could to strengthen my wrist and bring it back to its normal ability. On game day, I ended up playing again, and to top it off, we won! Being courageous, believing that I could overcome this challenging situation, and visualizing my success, definitely made a huge difference in my ability to be able to play again before the season ended. It was a miracle!*

**"We can either make ourselves miserable or we can make ourselves strong. The amount of work is the same."**
**~George Mumford~**
***The Mindful Athlete: Secrets to Pure Performance***

\* \* \*

**Iris:** Miracles happen when you least expect them! While you can't create a miracle, you can create the circumstances that will welcome them into your life. When you doubt, miracles typically don't happen. Visualization, affirmations, and feeling good are powerful signals to the Universe that you are on board and are ready to have magic enter into your life. Miracles happen when you believe and when you focus your energy on your goals and dreams in life. As Albert Einstein once said, *"There are only two ways to live your life. One is as though nothing is a miracle. The other is as though everything is a miracle."* Fear and faith cannot exist at the same time. You must choose which one will occupy your mind. If you choose to have faith, and believe anything is possible, then you will be living a life in the miracle zone. All you need to do is BELIEVE! And I believe in you! YOU CAN DO IT!

# Chapter 9

## Self-Care = Self-Love
by Jennifer Kauffman

*"How you treat yourself is how you are
inviting the world to treat you."*
~unknown~

**What is self-care?** *Self-care is anything that
nourishes your mind, body, and spirit. It's what we
instinctively and intentionally do to take care of
ourselves. Self-care keeps us in balance and improves
our mood, while reducing, and even eliminating,
anxiety and depression. Self-care is the fuel to our
vitality. It's vital to fostering good relationships with
ourselves and others. It's also important to
understand that self-care is not the same for everyone.
In other words, everyone has their own uniqueness,
so it's up to you to discover what self-care looks and
feels like to you. Also, what works for you today will
likely evolve as you continue to grow.*

***Self-care is not...*** *something we force upon ourselves, nor is it something we don't enjoy doing for ourselves. If you feel that something is draining or depressing, then it's a clue that you are not taking good care of yourself, and we encourage you to get help. Many people think self-care is a selfish thing to do, and they don't take the necessary time for it. This could not be further from the truth. The more we take care of ourselves, the more we have to give. Think of it like a bank account. Taking care of ourselves each day allows more and more of what I call "energy deposits" to be placed in our emotional bank account. When we are on the go all the time, we end up depleting our energy reserves, and as a result, we withdraw from our emotional bank account. The key is to have more in your emotional account than you use on a given day. The more you build up your emotional bank account, the easier life will become.*

**Self-care is an act of SELF-LOVE!**

*When we were infants and toddlers, we depended on others for our survival and love. At some point in our childhood, we start the transition of learning to take care of ourselves. For example, we learn to brush our teeth alone. We learn to bathe alone, and the list continues to build as we get older. Around the teenage years, most kids learn domestic chores, such as doing the dishes, making their bed, vacuuming the house, and possibly doing some light cooking. As you are busy mastering practical life skills, it's also essential to develop expanded self-care skills—which include acceptance, compassion, respect, empathy, resilience, forgiveness, and love—in order to truly thrive. The truth is, you will get hurt in life. Everyone does in some form or another. The point is to not live your life in fear. Remember, if you are not growing, you are slowly dying...it's up to you whether or not you expand and grow. The key is to embrace fear and to take action in the face of fear. Life is about the choices you make and how you respond in difficult times. Remember, you have the power within to respond like a victor. Or you can be a victim. The choice is all yours, and we encourage you to choose wisely.*

*The love we show to ourselves in the form of self-care will determine how far we go in life! Everything is energy, including you! Be mindful of the energy you are putting into the world. The more negativity you emit, the more it will come back to you. If you want more love and respect in your life, then give it to yourself first. For example, let's say a friend is disrespectful and rude to you. Do you simply allow it to happen and say nothing? If so, is it because you're too afraid to speak up and voice your truth? It takes courage to speak up in a loving and kind way. If you chose to respond with the same rudeness and disrespect that was given to you, then the situation will only escalate, and it never ends well! Someone* usually wins while the other loses. In this type of situation, you can speak your truth in a powerful, loving, kind way, simply by saying something like, "I feel hurt by what you just said." Or, "I don't appreciate being spoken to in that way." Or, "Did I do something to upset you?" If the negative behavior toward you continues, then it's up to you to decide whether this so-called friend stays in your life. Remember, we teach people how to treat us. If you do not want to tolerate this kind of behavior, then you simply walk away from the friendship in a peaceful manner. Remember, actions speak louder than words. When you let go of these friendships, it creates space for new ones to show up. And to be honest, these new friendships typically don't come rushing in. There's usually a gap, and within this gap is where you learn to be your very best friend and biggest cheerleader. Yes, it feels lonely, but I promise it's temporary, and it typically all works out for the best. Imagine and feel what it will be like when these new friends emerge. The more you do this, the quicker you'll attract them into your life!

Self-care is a daily practice. It's how you take care of your body, the foods you eat, and the people you surround yourself with. It's having a clean, tidy, and organized bedroom. Self-care means different things for different people. The objective is to define what self-care means to you. Here are some basic rules to follow:

**Just say no:** *Create a "no" list, with things you know you don't like or you no longer want to do. For example, you get to choose the friends that you let into your life. If you have promised to spend time with someone, and you realize that person is actually having a negative effect upon your life, you can change your mind; you are allowed to change your plans. Pay attention to when you are feeling pressured by friends—maybe they want you to see a movie that you are not comfortable seeing, or maybe they want you to spill secrets about another friend. The key is to follow your own heart. If you are not comfortable, speak up for yourself and say clearly that you don't want to do it. If you are unsure about your choice, or need help trying to figure out what to say about the situation, talk to an adult that you trust. They'll be able to help you.*

**Nutrition:** *Eat nutritious, colorful foods, which are filled with healthy vitamins and minerals. Limit the amount of junk food and sugar you eat. Too much sugar can cause mood swings, irritability, depression, weight gain, and even disease.*

**Sleep:** *For children and teens between the ages of 10 and 15, it is recommended that they get between 8 and 11 hours of sleep each night. Make sure that you are getting enough!*

**Rest**: *Be sure to get plenty of rest every day.*

**Spend time outdoors/play time:** *Get your body moving for at least 30 minutes a day. Exercise is good for your body and your emotional well-being. It increases serotonin levels (serotonin is the happy chemical in our body, which produces naturally when we exercise), leading to improved mood and energy. Find the type of exercise you enjoy doing...dancing, swimming, walking, biking, yoga, sports, etc.*

**Quiet time:** *Spend time being quiet each day, even if it is only for 5–10 minutes. You can do relaxation exercises, such as deep belly breathing, and/or practice meditation. Meditation has been linked to wellness.*

**Mind your thoughts:** *Watch what you believe...your beliefs lead to your thoughts, and your thoughts typically become your words. Watch your words, because they lead to your actions. Watch your actions, because they become your habits. Watch your habits, as they lead to your character. Your character determines your destiny. Your mind is like a muscle: The more you exercise it, by looking for the good in every situation, the stronger you will become.*

**Discuss your emotions:** *Your thoughts affect your emotions, and your emotions affect the choices you* make. *Always remember that the choices you make affect your life. Don't let your emotions distract you from always doing the right thing...being patient, loving, and kind. It is good to talk about your feelings. If someone has upset you, talk to them about it, in a kind and loving manner. Think of your emotions like a passing storm. If you resist or ignore your emotions, then they will linger longer...Simply allow your emotions to move through you.*

**Emotion** *is simply* **E***nergy in* **motion**

**Become your biggest cheerleader:** *Being your own cheerleader will enable you to continue to bring out the best of you in every situation. Even when you don't feel like being your own cheerleader, just remember that there is always someone looking up to you, so be the positive example that they need you to be!*

**Love:** *Spend time each day doing what you love...and tell the people in your life that you love them. Love raises your vibration and makes you feel good! Love is the answer for everything, and it sets you free to create a life your heart desires.*

**Happiness is an inside job:** *No one is in charge of your happiness. You are the only person who can make you happy! Your only job in life is to cultivate the happiness within YOU! Stop trying to please* *others; it only leads to disappointing yourself. You are in control of your own happiness. It does not come from the outside...when we take care of ourselves and do what makes us happy, it can disappoint others, but remember, that's their problem to solve. Someone else's disappointment is none of your business!*

***LOL:*** *Look for opportunities to laugh every day! Life is simply better when you're laughing, especially with those you love! Find time every day to simply LOL!*

*Set up a self-care routine, and notice how you feel better. And remember, self-care takes practice, so be patient, loving, and kind with yourself!*

> *"If you want to soar in your life,*
> *then you must learn how to F.L.Y.*
> ***F****irst* ***L****ove* ***Y****ourself."*
> *~Jennifer Kauffman~*

*Make a list of the things you love to do. Here are some self-care ideas to get you started (check all the ones that make you smile).*

### Self-Care Ideas

| | |
|---|---|
| ☐ Playing Games | ☐ Reading |
| ☐ Playing Sports | ☐ Writing |
| ☐ Dancing | ☐ Drawing |
| ☐ Singing | ☐ Painting |
| ☐ Playing a musical instrument | ☐ Arts & Crafts |
| | ☐ Making jewelry |
| ☐ Listening to music | ☐ Drama Class \| Theater |
| ☐ Writing music | ☐ Collaging |
| ☐ Watching a movie | ☐ Journaling |
| ☐ Riding your bike | ☐ Sleep over with friends |
| ☐ Going for a walk or hike | ☐ Telling funny jokes |
| ☐ Going swimming | ☐ Painting your nails |
| ☐ Going to the park or zoo | ☐ Building a tree fort |
| ☐ Cuddling with your pet | ☐ Taking a nap |
| ☐ Baking | ☐ Meditating |
| ☐ Cooking | ☐ Learning something new |
| ☐ Spending time with family & friends | ☐ Anything that makes you HAPPY! |

*It is up to you to break the cycle of victimhood and trauma. When you do not take extra good care of yourself, you are silently telling yourself that you are not worthy or good enough, which will only lead to a life of struggle.*

# Chapter 10

# Empowering YOU - A Reader's Guide
by Meghan, Kate, and Jennifer

*"The way out is the way through."*
~Robert Frost~

Meghan, Kate, and I are extremely grateful to be given the opportunity to learn from some extraordinary successful people, who've made such a profound difference in our lives. This chapter summarizes the key concepts that we've learned about living a courageous life. And we hope it will empower you to discover your best self, so that you, too, can live a life you love...free of trauma and struggle.

**#BeCourageous Key Concept #1: Accepting what is...**
The quicker you can accept what is, let go of what happened in your past, and have faith that everything is going to turn out for the best, the better off you'll be. You don't have to like what happened, but the longer you wish that something from your

past was different, the more you will stay stuck in your life. The key is to accept it, let it go, and learn to live in the present moment. Your power lies in the present, not in the past or the future. It's in the power of NOW.

**Yesterday is history,
tomorrow is a mystery,
today is a GIFT—that's why it's called
the PRESENT!**

If you are depressed, it's likely because you're living in the past or are stuck on a disempowering story about your life. If you are anxious, it's typically because you're worried about something in the future. If you are at peace with what is, then you know you are living in the present moment. When you find yourself distracted by your past, or worried about your future, stop and ask yourself, *"What am I grateful for in this moment?"* Another great way to empower yourself is to ask, *"Is what I'm concerned about going to come true with absolute certainty?"* Chances are the answer will almost always be NO. It's completely normal to feel fear when you are outside your comfort zone. Fear is nothing to be afraid of, even in a dangerous situation; you can always rise above your fear, take appropriate action, and remind yourself that this is another growth opportunity.

**#BeCourageous Key Concept #2: The choices YOU make will determine how high you soar in life!** Choice is one of the most powerful tools you have in life. You have the power within you to change your life at any time, simply by making different choices.

*Life is either a big daring adventure*
*or nothing at all.*

*It's either filled with an abundance*
*of success and failures*
*or nothing at all.*

*It's either filled with love, gratitude, and happiness,*
*or misery and struggle.*

*It all boils down to the CHOICES YOU make!*

Every word YOU speak, every action YOU take, all boils down to the choices YOU make. If you do not like the results in your life, remember that you have the power to change it, simply by choosing to say and do something differently!

**"Destiny is not a matter of chance;**
**it's a matter of CHOICE.**
**It's not a thing to be waited for;**
**it's a thing to be achieved."**
**~W.J. Bryan~**

| | | |
|---|---|---|
| **V** | Victors live <u>Above the Line</u>! | **C** |
| **I** | Victors take 100% responsibility | **H** |
| **C** | **O**wnership Victors see every challenge as an | **O** |
| **T** | **A**ccountability opportunity to expand and grow. | **I** |
| **O** | Victors easily forgive themselves & others. | **C** |
| **R** | **R**esponsibility Victors speak from "I..." | **E** |
| **S** | "I can see how you feel..." "I feel..." | **S** |

Victors live <u>Above the Line</u>!
Victors take 100% responsibility

**O**wnership

**A**ccountability
**R**esponsibility

Victors see every challenge as an
opportunity to expand and grow.
Victors easily forgive themselves & others.
Victors speak from "I..."
"I can see how you feel..." "I feel..."
Victors can go anywhere in life because
they use an OAR.

**O**wnership **A**ccountability **R**esponsibility

Victims live life <u>below the line.</u>
Victims are constantly whining,
complaining and blaming
everyone for their problems.

**B**lame

**E**xcuses

**D**enial

Victims point the finger at
everyone else and speak from
"You..." "You did this to me"...
Victims stand firm in...
"It's not my fault..."
"It's not my job..."
Victims spend a lot of time in BED!

**B**lame **E**xcuses **D**enial

V I C T O R S

C H O I C E S

V I C T I M S

J U S T I F Y

*Created by Jennifer Kauffman and inspired by Brad Sugars, Founder of Action Coach*

## #BeCourageous Key Concept #3: Stop being a victim! Rise up and become a VICTOR!

A person with a victim mentality is someone who constantly whines and complains about their life. Nothing is ever good enough for victims. They blame everyone for their problems, and they are difficult to be around. A victor is someone who embraces every challenge or problem they encounter, and sees it as positive because it is teaching them where they still have room to grow. If we are not growing, then we are slowly dying. Each day is an opportunity to expand and grow. Being around *victors* will help you grow faster. Victors support and encourage other victors. They are excellent at celebrating their progress and even their failures. They look at failure as a positive because, to them, it means they are attempting something new. Think of it like learning to ride a bike. You probably didn't just jump on your bike for the first time and ride it perfectly. Most likely, you fell repeatedly until you learned to balance yourself.

Move away from these disempowering victim questions...

- Why me?
- Why is this happening to me?

And replace them with these empowering victor questions...

- What is this experience attempting to teach me?
- What can I learn from this experience?
- What good can come from this experience?

**What do you choose to be? A** victim **or VICTOR?**

Here is something you can say to yourself when you're feeling discouraged and disempowered:

**"I shall always rise up! No matter how big the challenges are that I may face in my life, I will always find a way to rise up! I am the light! I am the fire inside of me who can burn through my challenges. And I will rise up more beautiful, loving, and stronger for having gone through this experience!"**
**~Jennifer Kauffman~**

**#BeCourageous Key Concept #4: Take 100% responsibility for your life!**

It doesn't matter how old you are; you can always take 100% responsibility. Taking 100% responsibility means that you have to give up all your reasons and excuses of why you can't or won't do something. Taking 100% responsibility decreases disagreements and increases happiness.

In Jack Canfield's best-selling book, *The Success Principles*, he highlights a key formula for living a successful life, which is known as:

**E+R=O**
**Events** in Your Life + Your **Response**
= **Outcomes** in Your Life

We cannot control the events that happen in our lives; however, we can control how we choose to respond to them, which in turn will determine our outcomes in life. It is entirely up to you to turn a bad situation into a growth opportunity. In Jack's book, he quotes George Washington Carver, a chemist who discovered over 300 ways to use a peanut. George said, *"99% of all failures come from people who have a habit of making excuses."* Do you make excuses in your life? We encourage you to STOP blaming, complaining, justifying, defending, and making excuses. We promise that you will not get very far in life if you choose to live this way. Remember, there are no "cannots;" there is only, "I choose not to!"

You can blame the event for your lack of results, but if you don't like your outcomes, you have the power within you to change your response to the event, which will create a different outcome.

**#BeCourageous Key Concept #5: Face your FEARs and RISE UP!**

Fear is a normal human emotion that is intended to be an alert. Think of a dashboard of a car that has alerts when the gas gauge is getting low, or the engine light comes on, signaling to pay attention. Fear is exactly the same; it's intended to heighten our awareness, and invites us to be vigilant about the fear we are choosing to face. Most people are afraid of their fears and do everything to avoid them. We've learned to embrace our fears because, when we do, we know they are ultimately helping us grow. Think of fear as:

**Face Everything And R** I S E

You are not going to completely alter your life in a single day. It requires mastering each day and living it to the fullest. It means creating new habits that will take you where you want to go in life. It requires you to be patient, persistent, loving, and kind with yourself. And the more you are grateful for your challenges, the easier it will be to tackle them.

**"RISE UP and be the best you can be, because the world is waiting for you to share your gifts."**
**~Jennifer Kauffman~**

**Take A Risk and GO FOR IT!**

**#BeCourageous Key Concept #6: Look for the GOOD in everything.**

Looking for good in everything is like looking for gold... it's rarely at the surface, and requires you to dig deep to find it! You are probably saying to yourself, "What good can come from losing a parent, a sibling, or a home, or from being bullied or surviving a horrific attack, like a mass school shooting? Let's be crystal clear: Nobody wishes to have these experiences in their lives, but the truth is that they are part of life. We cannot expand without having some sort of contraction. The key is to choose to look for the good in truly challenging situations. It is not easy at all, and often takes time before you begin to see the good in a bad situation. You have to rewire your brain to look for the good. Your brain is typically wired to look for the negative, so it takes time to rewire it. Be patient with yourself; it will eventually come.

I was standing 15 feet from a bomb that went off at the finish line of the 2013 Boston Marathon. I suffered all kinds of physical injuries, and was terrified of my own shadow. That event rocked me to my core. I felt completely shattered and had to learn how to rise up from that horrific experience.

Back in 2008, I received an award for consistently displaying gratitude. Gratitude was an important part of my daily life. However, in the early days of my recovery from the bombings, gratitude was the furthest thing from my mind. I was filled with tremendous fear. Over time, I began to remember the importance of being grateful, even though I struggled with it during my recovery. I began to realize that the more I expressed gratitude for the extraordinary doctors, practitioners, close family, friends, and complete strangers who came to my aid, the quicker I healed. One day, a close friend encouraged me to look for the good in that horrendous situation. I was stunned... *"Look for the good?"* I said, in a high pitched tone.

It was not easy for me to find the good in the beginning, but over time I started to see that there was so much good that came from that event. The more grateful and forgiving I became, the quicker I began to rise up, and heal from my injuries.

It has been six years since the bombings took place; and there were four years of intense physical, emotional, and spiritual healing, which eventually allowed me to rise up even stronger. In the past two years, I have written two best-selling books, and I am now working with my inspiring nieces on the third. I have produced a mission for a good film, *A New Leash on Life: The K9's for Warriors Story*, with the hope of saving more veterans' lives, who struggle with PTSD (post-traumatic stress disorder) and traumatic brain injury. This awe inspiring film has now won 4 Emmy awards. Nothing short of miraculous! If you asked me if I could imagine this during my recovery from the bombings, I'd tell you *absolutely not!* This horrific event turned out to be the greatest gift in my life. Sounds crazy, right? I learned so much about being grateful, especially in awful situations. I also learned the importance of forgiving everyone for everything, and the power of essential self-care, which led to my being able to heal naturally. I discovered that love is the way out of pain and suffering. Love is the medicine we all need. I found my way to rise up! If I can do it, so can YOU!

**#BeCourageous Key Concept #7: Letting go and forgiving everyone for everything!**

When you let go, you create space for something new and better to show up. It is never easy to let go, but it is unhealthy to hold on to negative feelings of anger, resentment, and sadness.

Here is an exercise you can do to demonstrate the power of letting go versus holding on:

- Pick up a pen in your non-dominant hand.
- Now, hold the pen as tight as you can...
- Just when you think you cannot hold it any tighter, I want you to squeeze even harder. Use your whole body if you have to...make sure you hold that pen as tight as you can!
- Now, hold onto that pen as tightly as you possibly can for at least 1 minute, or until your hand starts to shake or hurt...
- Then I want you to simply "let go" of the pen. Notice how you felt holding the pen...I bet it took a lot of energy, and it didn't feel good, did it? Now notice how you felt when you let go of the pen...Did it feel freeing to let it go?

Letting go and forgiving those that hurt you, whether they hurt you intentionally or unintentionally, will always set YOU free! Notice it's all about YOU, not them! Letting go and forgiving will immediately take you out of victimhood and will restore peace within YOU!

Forgiveness does not mean that you excuse the bad behavior. Forgiveness prevents the bad behavior from destroying YOU! Forgiveness is the highest form of love, and in return you'll receive peace and happiness within. There is no peace without forgiveness.

Often, we think that holding on makes us strong; but actually, letting go is what makes us stronger. Sometimes people never get what they want or deserve because they're too busy holding onto things they're supposed to let go of. One of the hardest lessons in life is letting go and moving on from things such as feelings of guilt, anger, loss, or betrayal. We fight to hold on, and we fight to let go. Change is never easy, and requires patience, kindness, and love.

**Holding on is often a struggle...**

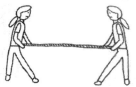

**Letting go can be hard, but it sets you free!**

**Practice forgiveness; it leads you to peace**. Here is a forgiveness exercise you can do. We encourage you to write a letter using the recommendations below:

- Tell your story in as much detail as possible.
- Express all your hurt.
- Grant forgiveness to the offender(s), and don't forget to include yourself, if necessary.
- Choose to either renew or release the relationship.
- You can either send the letter to the offender, if appropriate, or you can burn it.

The process of forgiveness is not forgetting or condoning what happened to you. It's about taking back your power and healing your life. Forgiveness literally sets you free and restores peace, love, and compassion within.

**"True forgiveness is when you can say,
Thank you for that experience."
~Oprah Winfrey~**

**#BeCourageous Key Concept #8: Develop an *attitude of gratitude*. Live everyday with gratitude!**

Gratitude brings us happiness. When you focus on gratitude every day, then all the disappointments in your life will simply begin to melt away. The vibration of gratitude attracts more abundance, positive opportunities, and incredible experiences into your life. Having an attitude of gratitude means that you choose to appreciate and value someone and/or something. Gratitude helps you recover more quickly from traumatic experiences in life. The more you express gratitude, either silently or out loud, the happier you become. Gratitude improves our relationships and leads to vitality.

**#BeCourageous Key Concept #9: To SOAR in life, you must learn to FLY.**

Your attitude about life will always determine your altitude in life!

It's time to spread your wings and F.L.Y. (First Love Yourself), so that you can let your spirit S.O.A.R. in life!

The body needs the spirit in the same way that a cell phone needs electricity: in order to function. For example, when you plug in a cell phone, the electricity is what brings the cell phone to life.

**"It takes courage to grow up
and become who you really are."
~E.E. Cummings~**

Our bodies are the same way. The more we raise our vibration, by choosing to be happy, loving, compassionate, forgiving, and kind, the better life will become. However, without electricity, the cell phone is dead, and so are we. We each have a spirit, and the spirit is the force that brings our body to life. Like electricity, the spirit has no feeling and cannot think. Spirit is a powerful and invisible force that is part of who we are. Without spirit—our life force—our bodies die, but our spirit stays alive, for it is eternal. The word, *spirit*, is sometimes referred to as the energy within.

We dare YOU to **F.L.Y.** (**F**irst **L**ove **Y**ourself) so that you can **S.O.A.R.** (**S**pirit **O**n **A** **R**ise in life!)

**#BeCourageous Key Concept #10: Use the power of your imagination to manifest your heart's desires...**

Imagination and visualization play a key role in being mindful. The more you visualize what you want, and allow yourself to feel what it would feel like when you achieve it, is how you are able to manifest your hearts desires more quickly. This is not something you do once. This is a daily practice, and it doesn't have to take a long time to do it each day.

**Your Imagination + Embody the Feelings of Reaching Your Goal + Massive Action = Dreams Fulfilled**

**"Logic will get you from A to B. Imagination will take you everywhere."**
**~Albert Einstein**

## How to Use Mindfulness and Positive Psychology/ Mindset to Be More Resilient

Positive psychology focuses on what allows people to thrive and function best. It teaches us ways to be more resilient and bounce back from adversities. Problems are nothing more than challenges to overcome, which help you grow! When you are solution focused you come up with new and creative ideas to move past the problem, this builds mental strength. It's the way our brain works. It concentrates on what we direct it toward, and we can direct it to be more solution focused instead of ruminating just on the problem we are facing.

Being mindful of our thoughts and shifting them to be more solution-focused is just one way to become more resilient. There are many other ways we can build up our resiliency "muscle". These include:

- Maintaining a positive self-image by focusing on our strengths and the skills and talents that we value
- Leaning on our faith and understanding the meaning of our purpose
- Having a mindfulness practice (like meditating) to help keep things in perspective and enable a positive outlook
- Practicing our problem-solving skills to increase adaptability
- Remembering self-regulation to help us control impulses
- Taking time to help others and keeping in touch with the people that are important to us

Positive psychology reminds us to pay attention to our strengths — these are our secret superpowers that can help us flourish in any situation — rather than our weaknesses to help us build confidence. It teaches us that no matter what happens in our lives that our perspective and mindset can help us reframe to see the good in life. Every single person is unique and the goal in life is to allow your uniqueness to shine. It is literally your gift to the world and you have the ability to make the world a better place.

You can become more aware of your strengths and how they can help you by taking the VIA Character

Strengths Survey. There is even a VIA Youth Survey for ages 10-17!

**Negative thinking *never* produces a positive life!**

All of your thoughts, feelings, and actions equal the results that you see in your life.   There are two versions to this formula. You get to choose the type of life you want, simply by deciding which formula to follow:

Negative Thoughts + Icky Feelings + Poor Decisions or Inaction = Disappointing Results
**or**
**Positive Thoughts + Uplifting Feelings + Massive Action = Miraculous Results**

**"Change your thinking. Change your life!**
**Your thoughts create your reality.**
**Practice positive thinking.**
**Act the way you want to be,**
**and soon you will be the way you act."**
**~Les Brown~**

**Life is Like a Mirror...**

And it will reflect back to you what you are thinking and feeling. Your life is a reflection of your beliefs and thoughts. If you want to change your life, start by changing your beliefs and thoughts, which will change your habits, and you'll start taking different actions.

If you find someone being disrespectful toward you, silently thank them—the truth is that they are giving you a gift to unwrap. Our tendency is to lash out with disrespect toward the person being disrespectful to us. Remember: Two wrongs don't make it right! Here's the gift in this situation, which requires you to focus your attention inwards by asking yourself, *"Where am I being disrespectful toward myself?"* Or if you feel that people do not accept you for who you are, then ask yourself, *"Where am I not fully accepting myself?"* If you feel whole, then you will not be triggered by what others say, either toward you or behind your back. You can't control their actions, but you can control your response—that is the power you have within you! The truth is, what others say about you is none of your business. The only thing that matters is how you see yourself!

**"Nothing brings me more joy than being able to do something that others said was impossible."**
**~Jennifer Kauffman~**

## #BeCourageous Key Concept #11: The power of focus and intention

When you focus on a thought, then your mind will move in the direction of that thought. When you consistently focus on what you want, day after day, then your life moves in that direction, as long as you take the required actions to expand your life. It does not come to you; you must take action to go get it.

When you are clear about your intentions, you will be inspired to take action that will be in alignment with your intentions. The more focused you are on what you want in your life, the more quickly you'll manifest your heart's desire. Think of intentions like a signal that is being sent out to the universe to be received. The stronger the signal—meaning the more you believe and embody the feeling that it's really going to happen, and then let go of any attachment of when—the faster it will show up. You must trust that the universe will provide it to you in the divine right timing, if it is meant for your highest good.

**"You are a living magnet.**
**What you attract into your life**
**is in harmony with your dominant thoughts."**
**~Brian Tracy~**

## #BeCourageous Key Concept #12: ASK

It takes a village to make a great life...one that is filled with love, happiness, adventure, and giving back. It simply requires you to ASK. We believe that ASKing is one of the keys to success.

**A**ccelerated **S**uccess **K**ey

Courageous questions to ASK yourself:

1. What is something you need to ask for?
2. Who do you need to ask?
3. How do you stop yourself from asking?
4. What is the cost of not asking?
5. What is the possible payoff if you were to ask?
6. When will you ask them?

**"You get in life what you have
the courage to ask for."
~Oprah Winfrey~**

ASK yourself, "What can I do today that will get me closer to where I want to be in the future?" When your inner peace, love, and happiness is disturbed...ask yourself, "What am I reacting to? What do I need right now?"

Surround yourself with people who have accomplished what you haven't yet, and ASK those questions that will help you learn as you find your own path. It takes more courage to ASK for help than it does to do it alone. Life is way more fun helping one another reach our hearts desires. The quality of your questions will determine the quality of your life. Successful people ask great questions, and as a result, they continue to expand and grow.

**Don't be afraid to ask...**
**If you do not ask, the answer will always be NO.**

If you ask, and the answer is no, that's okay...simply remember that a "no" means it wasn't in alignment with your highest good, and keep moving forward. When someone rejects you with a no, it is easy to think and feel like you are not good enough, but you have to realize that rejection is a sign that what you were asking for was not in your highest and best good. In other words, rejection is God's protection, or said another way, rejection is God's way of saying "wrong direction."

Surround yourself with people who encourage you and cheer you on, and who are willing to help you reach your dreams and goals in life.

## #BeCourageous Key Concept #13: Trust your vibes

Always trust your vibes. They are messages from your spirit; they are that inner part of you, which gives you everything you need. The truth is, you can never truly know another person; so, no matter what, ALWAYS trust your instincts. If everything seems fine on the surface, but alarm bells are going off inside, pay attention to the warning! We're all energetic beings, so if something doesn't feel right, trust it, and take appropriate action to get out of the situation.

**"If you want to learn to trust your vibes, you must maintain a peaceful and relatively calm attitude. When you're tense, nervous, or anxious, your energy gets tangled up and blocked, and can't enter your heart center, where your Higher Self and your vibes communicate."**
**~Sonia Choquette~**

**Trust your vibes...** *Energy* **does not lie!**

## #BeCourageous Key Concept #14: Energy is everything! Raise your vibration

Dr. Sue Morter, another one of my mentors, describes the Five Energy Code Truths, which are:

1. Everything is ENERGY.
2. Your life is a reflection of your ENERGY.
3. You are the creator of your life.
4. Your creation—your life—is always expanding.
5. The purpose of your life is to discover your creatorship.

You are either raising your energy up or allowing it to spiral down with your emotions. This diagram illustrates that your vibration determines what you attract into your life. Remember that you are the creator of your life.

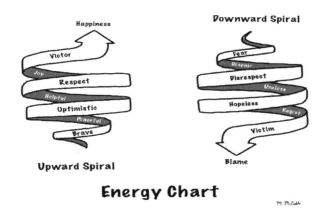

**Energy Chart**

**#BeCourageous Key Concept #15: Self-care = Self-love**

Self-care is essential and includes anything you'd do to be good to yourself. It's about being patient, kind, and loving to yourself, just like you'd be toward others. It's knowing when your energy reserves are running low, and being willing to take a timeout from your fast-paced, busy life to replenish your energy in whatever way serves you best. Self-care means eating well, getting plenty of rest, and moving your body every day! Discover what you love, and do more of it! Refer to the self-care checklist, in chapter 10, for ideas, and we encourage you to make your own list. Self-care is all about learning how to F.L.Y.

**F**irst **L**ove **Y**ourself!

**#BeCourageous Key Concept #16: Simply love for no reason, be happy for no reason, and learn to live your life in the miracle zone...**

Kate and Meghan were so happy to meet and learn from one of my mentors, Marci Shimoff, who is an expert on happiness, success, and unconditional love. During their interview with Marci, they learned so much about what it takes to be happy and love for no reason. Here is a summary of Marci's steps for loving for no reason, being happy for no reason, and learning to live a life in the miracle zone:

**Love for No Reason – 7 Steps to Creating a Life of Unconditional Love**

1. **The Doorway of Safety: Being in the Here and Now**
   The key is to enjoy life living in the present moment. When you are in the present, each moment becomes a gift!

2. **The Doorway of Vitality: Turning up the Juice**
   Raising Your Vibration. Be the *energy* you want to attract in your life!

3. **The Doorway of Unconditional Self-Love: Loving Yourself No Matter What...**
   Tame your inner critic and learn to love the part of you that you think is unlovable. The more you learn to love yourself and others unconditionally, the more amazing your life will be.

4. **The Doorway of Openness: Living with an Open Heart**
   Lean into being compassionate with yourself and others.
   Perform random acts of kindness.
   Give *free* hugs.

5. **The Doorway of Communication: Coming from Compassion**

When someone triggers strong emotions, simply pause, and take a deep breath. Learn to speak loving and kind words in triggering situations.

6. **The Doorway of Vision: Seeing with the Eyes of Love**

Train your eyes to look for the beauty in everything.

Trust your instincts, which is your inner wisdom directing you to the right path for you.

7. **The Doorway of Oneness: Connecting to Wholeness**

Surrender to what is and communicate to the divine.

**Happy for No Reason – 7 Steps to Being Happy from the Inside Out**

1. **The Foundation: Take Ownership of Your Happiness**

Focus on a solution, not the problem.

Look for the lesson and gift in all experiences.

Make peace with yourself.

**2. The Pillar of the Mind: Don't Believe Everything You Think**
Question Your Thoughts...Always remember, YOU have the power to change them.
Focus your mind on joy.

**3. The Pillar of the Heart: Let Love Lead**
Focus on gratitude.
Practice forgiveness.
Spread love and kindness everywhere you go.

**4. The Pillar of the Body: Make Your Cells Happy**
Nourish your body with whole foods.
Energize your body. Do some form of exercise each day. Our bodies are meant to move.

**5. The Pillar of the Soul: Plug Yourself in to Spirit**
Listen to your inner voice.
Trust your instincts, and connect with your higher power.

**6. The Roof: Live a Life Inspired by Purpose**
Find your passions in life.
Follow the inspiration of the present moment.
Contribute or give back to something greater than yourself.

7. **The Garden: Cultivate Nourishing Relationships**
   Surround yourself with encouraging, supportive, and loving people. Choose to see the world as your friend, constantly giving you opportunities to expand and grow.

**3 Steps to Living Your Life in the MIRACLE ZONE**

1. Create from your soul intention rather than your ego intention.
   *"I want to lose 20 lbs." has an ego vibration to it. The soul intention would be: "I am fit, vibrant, and healthy in the body that reflects the soul that I am."* The energetic perspective you have, while you are creating, has a huge impact on your ability to manifest, and Marci says that when you manifest from your soul intention rather than from your ego, that is when you enter the miracle zone.

2. Live from the heart, instead of the mind.

3. Feel worthy! If you are not feeling worthy, stop and ask yourself what you could do for yourself right now that is loving. How can you open yourself to receiving more today?

## What does it mean to live your life in the miracle zone?

Simply be curious and open to unexpected miracles showing up in your life each day. Miracles come in all shapes and sizes. It might be finding a parking spot in a full parking lot; it might be getting an unexpected phone call from a friend, asking you to do something fun; or it might be getting an 'A' on your exam, when you thought you did poorly.

**#BeCourageous Key Concept #17: Just say YES to Success...**

Meghan and Kate were so excited to meet another one of my mentors, Debra Poneman, founder of the YES to Success program. Debra teaches that success isn't about having lots of money or lots of stuff. Success is about how you positively impact another person's life. Success is about helping one another reach new heights. Success isn't meant to be competitive, where someone wins and someone loses. Success is an opportunity to expand and grow.

### *What does success mean to you?*

Believing in yourself is the first secret to success. You're successful as soon as you start to move toward your hearts desires. Success is not about how much money you make; instead, it's about the profound difference you are willing to make in the lives of others. This is the cool acronym I came up with for success:

**S** tart now
**U** nwavering
**C** ommitment
**C** onsistency
**E** nergy
**S** elf-discipline
**S** implicity

The key to success is to STOP spending time on your obstacles, and spend more time focusing on your goals and dreams! Success is only possible when you take consistent actions in the direction you want your life to go...Successful people fail and make mistakes, but they never quit!

**"You'll never change your life**
**until you change something you do daily.**
**The secret of your success is found**
**in your daily routine."**
**~John C. Maxwell~**

Create win-win opportunities, especially when you have differing opinions. It is healthy to have your own personal opinion, and it is also healthy for others to have theirs. The opportunity is to look for common ground, where you both can find a workable solution, where everyone wins.

## Life is about creating WIN WIN situations!

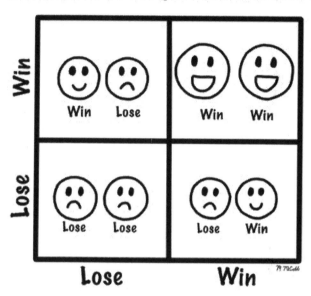

**#BeCourageous Key Concept #18: The power of *yet***

There is a difference in not knowing and not being able to achieve something...yet. *Yet* is a powerful word, and it encourages us to keep moving forward. When you learned to walk, you did not walk perfectly the moment you stood up. You stumbled and fell, over and over, until you mastered walking. The key is to keep getting up until you reach your goal. Strength doesn't come from what you can do...it comes from overcoming things that you once couldn't do. Learn to develop a growth mindset, instead of saying things like...

*I'm not good at...*
*This is too hard...*
*I just can't do this...*
*I give up!*

Consider thinking differently by asking yourself a few powerful questions and saying some empowering statements like...

*What am I missing?*
*Am I really giving it my all?*
*Am I doing my best?*
*I can always improve!*
*Mistakes help me learn!*
*FAIL simply means First Attempt In Learning.*

**#BeCourageous Key Concept #19: Just remember HI! Honesty and Integrity**

**What is Integrity?** Integrity is being honest and ethical. It means doing the right thing and honoring your commitments to yourself and others. The truth is, everyone makes mistakes. It takes honesty and integrity to own up to them.

**"Being honest may not get you a lot of friends,
but it'll always get you the right ones."**
**~John Lennon~**

**Be honest, speak your truth,
and always DO the right thing!**

**#BeCourageous Key Concept #20: To expand and
GROW, you must keep going outside your comfort
zone...**

Living in your comfort zone will not get you very far
in life...Life is meant to be lived just outside your
comfort zone. When we go just beyond our comfort
zone, that's when we expand and grow. Let's be clear:
This is not meant to push yourself so far outside your
comfort zone that you can't handle it. The point is to
go to *your edge*. It's where you will feel a mixture of
fear and excitement, and where you'll be able to take
steps to move forward. Notice that we said, *your* edge!
Never compare yourself to someone else's edge.
Comparing yourself to another person will
continuously set you up for failure and frustration.
Simply find your edge, and break through your fear
so that YOU can expand and grow!

Let's use the example of someone being afraid of
heights. You would not encourage them to go sky
diving if they can barely walk up a flight of stairs. In

this example, their edge may be getting to the top of a 3-story building, and once they get comfortable with that, we'd encourage them to determine what the next step is in order to go beyond their fear of heights...It could be going to the top of a 5-story building. The key is to keep expanding your comfort zone. When you expand your comfort zone, life will get more and more exciting, and your confidence will increase too. Not to mention, new opportunities will show up so that you can continue to expand and grow.

Every day, do something outside your comfort zone that helps you grow! It could be standing up to a bully. It could be telling someone that they hurt your feelings. It could be learning something new, where you might fail or look foolish. Going outside your own boundaries is the key to living an expansive, successful life.

**"It is impossible to live without failing at something, unless you live so cautiously that you might as well not have lived at all, in which case you have failed by default."**
**~J.K. Rowling~**

## #BeCourageous Key Concept #21: Giving back

Giving back is a vital ingredient to living a courageous and successful life. When we help those less fortunate than ourselves, we help them rise up...The more we help each other rise, the more we'll all be able to make the world a better place!

Giving back is simply good for our health. When we feel good, we release happy chemicals in our bodies. These happy chemicals improve our immune system and the overall functioning of our bodies. Giving back isn't just about giving money. It can mean helping a neighbor in need or volunteering at a shelter, or cleaning up a park, or reading your favorite story to people living in nursing homes.

**"At the end of life, we will not be judged
by how many diplomas we have received,
how much money we have made,
how many great things we have done.
We will be judged by
"I was hungry,
and you gave me something to eat,
I was naked and you clothed me.
I was homeless, and you took me in."
~Mother Teresa~**

## Unleashing Courageous YOU

If you have to sneak it, don't do it; if you have to lie to cover it up, don't do it; and if you have to delete it from being seen, then don't do it! Always be the best YOU can be! Be kind, especially when you don't want to. Be understanding even when you're angry. Do more than you have been asked to do, and don't expect anything in return. God gave us two ears to listen and one mouth to speak...So listen fully when someone talks, and don't interrupt them! Simply respond when they are done. Tell people every day how much you love and appreciate them! Before going to bed, take a few minutes to acknowledge what you are grateful for. And when you wake up in the morning, give thanks for another day, and be sure to set your positive intentions for the day. Remember, we create our reality with our thoughts. If you think you'll have a bad day, then you will. However, if you think you'll have a miraculous day, then you will. Go out of your way to help those in need. Giving back will fill your heart with an abundance of love, and it helps those less fortunate rise up. Giving back and helping others makes the world a better place! Be the greatest person you can be, every day, and when you mess up (And you will. We are imperfect human beings; embrace your imperfections.), take 100% responsibility, apologize, forgive yourself, and move on. The quicker you can do this, the quicker you will bounce back. Think of life like a bike: To balance, you must keep moving forward.

Never spend time trying to prove yourself to anyone. Stop trying to please others; it will only lead to a life of struggles, suffering, and misery. Remember that your actions will always speak louder than your words. If someone does not like you, that says more about them than about you. Remember, like attracts like. Sometimes our light is simply too bright for those who choose to live in darkness. But no matter what...

**Never stop shining your light brightly in this world!!**

Now it's time for you to go out to create and live a life you love! You have everything you need to get started! We believe you can do it! The sky is the limit for you! Keep reaching for the stars! Shine your light brightly in this world, and always LOVE more...

Our wish for you is that you are inspired and encouraged enough to take the first step. The truth is that everyone goes through extremely difficult times, and when you stop to remember that these challenging times are meant to strengthen you, and to teach you to rise up even stronger, then it will make your journey a little easier. Everything that happens in life is teaching us to love ourselves and others more. Love is the answer! Love is the way out of pain and suffering. Forgiveness sets you free! Stop being a victim, and become a courageous victor in life!

We wish you a life filled with an abundance of peace, love, joy, happiness, adventure, and FUN!!

**"RISE UP and embrace each day with ENTHUSIASM."**
**~Jennifer Kauffman~**

**#BeCourageous NOW!**

# Bonuses

To obtain the free bonuses that go along with this book, please visit www.becourageousbook.com.

Download your free copy of **"A Friend's Guide to Dealing with Challenging Experiences,"** which is a tool designed for friends who know people who've been affected by a traumatic experience. This guide will provide you with tips and strategies to help you support your friend in an empowering, loving, and encouraging way.

Download your free copy of **"A Siblings Guide to Dealing with Difficult Times,"** which is a tool designed for brothers and sisters who have a sibling who has gone through a traumatic experience. This guide will provide you with tips and strategies to help you support your sibling in a hopeful, uplifting, and loving way.

Download your free copy of **"A Parent's Guide to Helping Children Who Have Gone Through a Traumatic Experience."** This guide is a parent's perspective on trauma, and it will provide you with tips and strategies to help you best support your children in rising up from trauma.

To download your free copy of **"Create Your Own Self-Care Check List,"** please go to www.becourageousbook.com.

To learn about the **"7 Laws of the Universe – A Guide to Living Your Best Life,"** please go to www.becourageousbook.com to download a free copy.

Made in the USA
Lexington, KY
26 November 2019